The
Corporate
Athlete

Advantage

The Science of
Deepening Engagement

Dr. Jim Loehr and Dr. Jack Groppel

A Human Performance Institute Publication
Human Performance Institute
9757 Lake Nona Road
Orlando, Florida 32827
+1 (1) 407.438.9911
www.corporateathlete.com

The Corporate Athlete Advantage: The Science of Deepening Engagement

Edited by Renate J. Gaisser

Manufactured in the United States of America

Library of Congress Cataloging-in-Publication Data is available upon request.

ISBN: 978-0-9778776-5-2

October 2008
First Edition

Featured Contributors:

Chris Osorio

Raquel Malo

Chris Jordan

Dr. Leo Greenstone

Alan McMillan

Fred Harburg

Jenny Evans

Jim Mellado

Rear Admiral Ray Smith

Will Marre

Contents

Why the Corporate Athlete® Advantage

by Dr. Jim Loehr and Dr. Jack Groppel

We hold ourselves accountable for how we spend our time and our money. Someone who doesn't monitor and marshal these resources would likely be considered wasteful, undisciplined and unprofessional. But what about how we spend that other precious resource, the one that, we contend, is even more valuable to us than time or money—our energy? Do we hold ourselves accountable for our energy expenditure? Do we ever stop to consider how it is that we can consistently ignore the simplest of equations—namely energy in equals energy out? And what happens when energy deposits do not keep pace with energy withdrawals? From decades of data collection, we at the Human Performance Institute (HPI) have found the answer lies in progressive and deepening disengagement at work, at home, in life.

For more than a quarter-century, our "solution" to this problem has helped corporations and other organizations, including those in areas as disparate as medicine and law enforcement, to increase the productivity, health and happiness of their constituencies. Our solution trains high performers to stop exclusively focusing on managing a non-expandable resource—time—and to start focusing on managing a resource that clearly can be expanded—energy. Our *Corporate*

Athlete Advantage, which has evolved over many years of collaboration, helps high-level performers to more skillfully manage their energy (physical, emotional, mental and spiritual) in much the same way that highly successful professional athletes must. Time and again we have seen how skillful management of energy leads to increased levels of employee engagement at work and at home. Increased engagement, in turn, positively impacts work performance, healthcare costs, turnover rate and absenteeism—to name just a few crucial business yardsticks.

Though our concept of *energy management* is, most importantly, grounded in science, it also possesses a strong "common sense" element. According to HPI's longitudinal data collection as well as data collected by our clients, high-level performers who graduate from the training find it to be transformative and, for some, life changing. For almost all of us, it seems that every year we have more responsibilities and are expected to execute them using fewer resources. The fundamental question we pose to those who attend the executive course at the Human Performance Institute in Orlando, Florida, the U.S. Olympic Training Center in Colorado Springs, Colorado and at off-site locations around the world, is this:

How will you meet the ever-increasing demands in your life?

Some answer it by telling themselves they will learn to multitask better. Others say, "Sure, it can be done—but only," they acknowledge, "by putting other things such as family and health on the backburner, while the new demands are met." Others believe they will solve it by managing their time more efficiently. In fact, most clients answer the question by saying something like, "If I have to do more work, then I will somehow have to find a way to allocate more time to it."

Most of us have already figured out that these solutions are tragically inadequate. They simply don't work. They can't work. Because time is finite, so is its ability to help us. What happens to the quality of our work when we multitask? What are the real consequences of compromising energy with our families or our health over and over again? Where do we take the time from? It has to come from something else, or someone else, because time is fixed, non-expandable. If we follow the "time management" solution, then we will inevitably take time away from something extremely important, most often family, friends, community service or time for personal renewal. That's simply not an acceptable strategy when considering our deepest values.

So why does the corporate athlete solution work? It works because it's founded on the acknowledgement that the fundamental currency of life, both personal and professional, is energy. Without energy, every cause is lost, every mission, however noble, is doomed to failure.

To start, we believe that far too many high-stress arenas such as the world of business wrongly assume that the human body is not "performance-relevant." Let's look at the corporate world. The corporate athlete solution is premised on the idea that the body most certainly *is* performance-relevant because it is, in fact, the physical body itself that produces all the energy required to drive each and every business function. Indeed, we also firmly believe that the corporate athlete solution can have a significant impact on the healthcare problem worldwide. (A problem for which the business world is, in many ways, partially responsible.) For years, demand on employees has increased. Year after year, workers must adapt to the pressure of increasing expectations, productivity and profitability. If asked, business leaders across the board will proudly say that they recognize the need for their people to take care of themselves. Yet invariably their organizations struggle for practical solutions to help workers achieve healthier lifestyles.

Today's leaders clearly recognize that the rising cost of healthcare is reducing corporate profitability. Poor morale, low motivation, burnout and retraining costs are just a few of the eventual consequences of poor health. Inactivity, obesity, poor nutrition and unhealthy eating habits are common place in corporate life. Given these factors (and more), we believe that business leaders make a critical mistake by not considering the body in the formula of high performance.

So why do we rely so heavily on the world of sport science for building our model of energy management? We do so for a number of reasons. First, our backgrounds willed it. We are both committed to solutions based on solid science. Jack trained in biomechanics and exercise physiology. His study of nutrition naturally viewed performance through the physiological lens of science. Jim's training in psychology instinctively led him to look to the world of psychological science for improving performance. The more experience each of us gained separately in our specialty areas, however, the more convinced we became that the best way to raise performance levels was to create a seamless integration of all the sciences, most importantly the sport sciences because the focus is primarily on human performance. The most effective model of performance, we argued, would be the one that most accurately reflected the way the human being was designed—a fully integrated, multi-dimensional energy system. With that goal in mind, we set out to combine all the sport sciences under the single umbrella of energy management.

Here was our logic. In tennis, for example, getting the ball to go from point A to point B with a certain spin and speed represented a complex energy management challenge. Involved in the energy equation were physical issues of biomechanics, movement, strength, flexibility, fitness, hydration, sleep, nutrition and overall physical health as well as psychological issues of concentration, motivation, confidence, relaxation, enjoyment, the presence of fear or anger, emotional resiliency and mental toughness. The performance formula involved physical energy, emotional energy, mental energy and something we came to refer to as spiritual energy, the energy of purpose. The increasing experience we had, coupled with the data we collected from our clients, further corroborated that, be it in the world of professional sport or business, using energy as the central organizing principle offered distinct and significant advantages. For us, the most important questions to ask were these: (1) How does diet, fitness, sleep, hydration, confidence, focus, emotional state, motivation, etc. affect one's energy state at any given time? And (2) how can one train to manage energy more skillfully in the various dimensions in an effort to achieve maximum performance?

Applying sport science research to the world of business serves another purpose. Corporate employees will see that the principles that govern an athlete's success are rather analogous to those that govern their success. We want corporate employees to compare how they manage energy with what world-class athletes learn to do. Elite athletes revere their bodies. They fully understand that without a healthy body, all their dreams of success come to a screeching halt.

In top-class athletics, it's unthinkable *not* to consider the body as one plots a road to success. Can you imagine a professional athlete preparing for a big event by scarfing down some fast food, fries and a sugary soft drink just before heading onto the field? Or by getting a couple hours of sleep every night for the previous two weeks? If he or she did that, what would it do to his or her energy level, physiology and readiness to perform? Such practices would eventually undermine their careers. No serious athlete would be so careless and unprofessional when preparing to perform.

Yet the business executive does that and more without even giving it a second thought. In all too many organizations, it's actually counter-culture to be physically fit, to eat healthy foods and to follow clearly defined health rituals on a regular basis.

Let's compare the professional lives of world-class athletes and business executives, referred to as corporate athletes in our training. World-class athletes train as much as 90 percent of the time. They perform and compete very little; as little as 10 percent of the time they are truly held accountable. Corporate athletes, on the other hand, perform, compete and are held accountable virtually 100 percent of the time; they train very little. Athletes have coaches who support proper eating, sleeping, fitness, recovery and rest. Corporate athletes have no such luxury. Extending the analogy still further, athletes on many team sports have lengthy off-seasons, as much as three to four months, or even more. As corporate athletes, when is our off-season? (Off-season? Frequently we are fighting for a *weekend*.) Like top athletes, corporate athletes need energy, lots of it. Unlike top athletes, corporate athletes need energy not for a career span of five to seven years as in professional sport but rather for 30 to 40 years. To top it off, the corporate athlete (though this is true of many others, too) often arrives home to family awaiting his or her arrival; they, too, demand much of the corporate athlete's energy, and deserve it. The fact is that, considering everything, there are more demands for energy on corporate athletes than any athlete we have ever worked with. That comes as quite a shock to our corporate clients.

And, as we said earlier, the demands in business and in life continue to soar. We routinely hear Chief Executive Officers (CEOs) say things like, "In the future, decisions must be made faster, thinking must be more streamlined, vertical communication must improve, personal responsibility and accountability must be taken more seriously, technology, IT systems, information sources and outsourcing must improve and be better exploited, cross-functional activities must be more efficient, and individuals at all levels of the corporation must feel empowered. In short, everyone needs to step up and do more."

According to data we have collected over many years from thousands of executives and high-level performers from medicine, sport and military venues, the greatest stressors include:

1. The relentless expectations to do more and more with fewer resources.
2. The lack of depth in life at work and at home. Stretched so thin they feel a mile wide and a half inch deep.
3. Fatigue that compromises their ability to be fully present with family and loved ones as well as fully present at work.
4. Crisis of purpose—lack of meaning and significance in their lives, disconnection between their personal and professional lives.
5. Compromised health and personal happiness. The demands and pressure of work are so excessive they fear they may lose two of the things that are most precious to them—their personal health and sense of well-being in life.

The word that best captures what high-level performers are up against, and what is causing dissatisfaction is *disengagement*. Disengagement from family, from health, from feelings of significance, from depth in their lives, from feelings of fulfillment and personal happiness, and from feelings of excitement and high energy. That is precisely why we make the central organizing principle in all of our training at the Human Performance Institute that of *engagement*.

When will high-stress performers be asked to do less? For as long as they choose to stay in the game, expectations to do more will increase every year. And that means longer work hours, less time for exercise, less time for healthy eating. In other words, the foundation of incoming energy—good nutrition, regular physical activity, proper rest—are all even further threatened. While we constantly pursue "energy out," as if by sheer desire, our will allows our bodies to out-smart basic physics. Again, considering the athlete's scenario, think of Olympic speed skating gold medalist Bonnie Blair. What would have happened to her performance if she so blatantly had ignored her body's physical demands? Clearly there would be significant per-formance consequences over time. Her chosen career would be in serious jeopardy.

For all our tremendous respect for the professional athletes with whom we have worked—and for professional athletes in general—we discovered, much to our surprise, that corporate athletes and medical athletes are under more constant pressure, have higher con-sequences for failure and more demands on their energy; further-more, they perceive that there is never time for themselves. Though the need for stamina may be more conspicuous in the case of pro-fessional athletes, a corporate executive or surgeon needs as much stamina as a professional athlete to perform at highly competent lev-els under intense pressure for 10 or more hours a day, often six days a week. As already pointed out, corporate and medical athletes are expected to continue this extraordinary output over a career span of possibly four decades.

So how can "athletes" not from the world of sport maintain that competitive edge for bottom-line improvement? How can a corpo-rate athlete achieve maximal performance—whether negotiating a sale, building a high-performance team or making their numbers? Corporate athletes must handle pressure at work, perform on de-mand regardless of circumstances, access their talent and skills when they need them most, manage their time efficiently, and set realistic goals and expectations for themselves. In short, they must be on at all times—no excuses! It's no stretch, then, to see the "non-athlete" from the high-stress worlds of business, medicine and law enforce-ment as the "ultimate athlete." The real question is whether they are training like one!

The uniqueness of the corporate athlete solution—compared to other training and development programs—is that we acknowledge how individuals are holistically designed. Performers come to work with bodies, emotions, minds and spirits. They are innately fully integrat-ed—that is, their bodies are not disconnected from their feelings, thoughts, values and beliefs, no matter how fervently we may wish it were so. The energy reserve of the business executive or medical professional is rarely a target for training and development. Taking care of the body is simply not regarded as sufficiently performance-relevant to justify the investment of serious training dollars. Health and wellness initiatives in the world of business are rarely borne of concerns for the energy reserves of employees, or recognition that the low energy levels of employees compromise all business functions. Health and wellness programs are rarely viewed as core business imperatives but rather employee perks that simply serve to increase the costs of employee benefit packages. Clearly, making the connection between business success and energy renewal physically, emotionally, mentally and spiritually remains beyond the scope of almost all prevailing business models.

This book is about what can happen when leaders begin with a performance model that fully embraces the reality that workers are fully integrated, multi-dimensional energy systems. It explores the implications and ramifications for establishing energy as the sine qua non currency of high performance. It analyzes the unique and practical solutions that our corporate athlete model brings to problems of employee engagement, escalating employee healthcare costs, employee safety concerns, turnover, work/life balance issues and great-place-to-work initiatives.

Chris Osorio will introduce the Human Performance Institute's business objectives with our clients, and then provide a few examples of our successful relationships with clients. The *Principles* section of the book starts with Jim Loehr highlighting the foundational components of our corporate athlete solution (*Chapter 1*), covering principles from the oscillatory nature of our energy and engagement patterns, to accurately measuring the various dimensions of energy for assessing engagement levels. In *Chapter 2*, Raquel Malo, our lead nutritionist, briefly describes the role food intake has on our ability to engage and perform at our best, and recounts different "stories" we may tell ourselves about food that undermine our ability to follow energy-optimizing eating habits. The last chapter of the *Principles* section, *Chapter 3*, is dedicated to the function of movement, exercise and recovery in staying engaged. Chris Jordan also imparts some of the cycles that, if followed, help maximize engagement from a movement perspective.

Part II of the book, entitled *Applications*, is a compilation of relevant sectors in which the implications of the energy management principles have been—or very well could be—used to benefit its respective constituents. Jack Groppel opens this section with a compelling case for a departure from the corporate status quo pertaining to how stress is viewed and treated, sharing some statistics about the consequences of stress, and offering the corporate athlete solution as a unique and practical solution to the conditions that render high energy and high performance unsustainable. *Chapter 5*, authored by Dr. Leo Greenstone, furthers the case for the effectiveness of the corporate athlete solution, this time from the healthcare perspective. He posits that by incorporating energy management principles into our organizations and communities, we could significantly reduce healthcare costs while increasing productivity from our workers.

Alan McMillan then shares his experience with how the corporate athlete solution has benefited him and others within the National Safety Council, personally and in furthering the mission of their organization. His belief is that the principles of the corporate athlete solution have been able to create a safer and healthier environment for the 21st Century workforce, both at work and at home. In *Chapter 7*, Fred Harburg outlines an approach for Chief Learning Officers to successfully implement change within an organization, an approach that is analogous to that presented in the corporate athlete solution. By overlaying the two, he shows that the corporate athlete solution would be an effective tool in any organization that desires to be competitive in their respective, often volatile industry.

Jenny Evans provides a glimpse at the power of storytelling, a key principle of the corporate athlete solution, as she relays her journey over time regarding self-views as manifested in her quest to define what it means to be an "athlete." By incorporating the rituals inherent in the corporate athlete model, she has crafted a story that supports continued improvement in all aspects of her life. *Chapters 9* and *10* both express the benefits of the energy management principles in better executing missions, albeit very different missions. Jim Mellado speaks of his enhanced ability to be a leader—religious leader, that is—highlighting the importance of taking care of one's physical body and one's ability to be fully engaged® in taking on the emotional, mental and spiritual demands associated with religious leadership. Rear Admiral Ray Smith, then, describes how the energy management principles form the exact formula for Navy SEAL mission success. In the final chapter of this book, Will Marre establishes the need for the corporate athlete solution in the corporate world today: In order to remain competitive, organizations need the very best talent to be functioning at optimal levels. The innovation and engagement required for this to be achievable is through implementing the principles of the corporate athlete solution into the work culture.

These applications serve as an indicator of the wide and extensive benefits that those who implement the corporate athlete solution will find in their work lives, personal lives and as members of their communities.

Getting Acquainted With the Human Performance Institute

by Chris Osorio

O n a spring day in 2002, my office phone rang. On the other end of the line was my friend Will Marre, Covey Leadership Center's charismatic Co-founder and initial President. Will was scouting firms to bring executive education to one of his corporate clients, and while searching he stumbled upon an innovative firm—the Orlando-based Human Performance Institute. Will thought HPI might be the organization to provide his client with what they needed. He was captivated even more by the revolutionary theory of managing one's energy.

To be sure, Will is almost terminally enthusiastic; but as his words spilled out, I could tell that, even for him, he had found something special. He had seen the "next big thing" in training and development, an entirely new category of training and equally, if not more, important than the entire field of time management training, which FranklinCovey had become famous for.

Will told me that the firm was founded by Dr. Jim Loehr and Dr. Jack Groppel. He spoke of Jim much as he had always spoken of Dr. Stephen R. Covey, former CEO of the Covey Leadership Center and one of the finest leaders in the training and development (T&D) industry. Jim was a pioneer in the field of performance psychology, one of the most prominent theorists and practicing sport psychologists in the world, and a prolific writer in his field—with a client list that reads like a Who's Who of sport. He, in fact, continues to be sought out by the world's best athletes from all dimensions of sport, consulting with them on how to improve their performance, and is an active member on the highly selective U.S. Olympic Committee's Sport Psychology Registry.

I already knew, if only a little, of Jack Groppel; an exercise physiologist and nutritionist who had performed pioneering work in biomechanics. I would later find out that he is a Fellow in the American College of Sports Medicine, served for 16 years as the Chairman of the U.S. Tennis Association's National Sport Science Committee and is currently on the National Board of Directors of the U.S. Professional Tennis Association. But I first encountered Jack when he spoke in front of 20,000 people at the then Delta Center—now Energy-Solutions Arena—in Salt Lake City, a presentation I had heard and remembered well because Jack, with his persuasive data and inescapable logic, had stolen the day from a list of distinguished speakers.

What Jim Loehr and Jack Groppel were doing at the Human Performance Institute, Will told me, was unique and fundamental, and their message both timely and timeless. What they had learned about performance and productivity, health and happiness, and how they were communicating that to clients, was something everyone needed to hear.

Yet HPI appeared to lack business leadership. Therefore Will suggested we do some due diligence on them, if I was to pursue a relationship with them. Along with Dr. Stephen M.R. Covey, my other most trusted professional colleague, we three went deeper with our review of HPI.

I had seen many promising boutique shops fail to grow past the incubation stage, so I was initially skeptical about HPI. During my ten years at the Covey Leadership Center, I had been fortunate enough to be part of a sensational team that had grown a US$3 million boutique consulting shop into a US$500 million training and development (T&D) enterprise. But that was clearly an exception.

It wasn't long into our research on HPI that we realized we were dealing with something special. Of the many notable things about Jim and Jack, perhaps this impressed us most. Early in their careers as performance coaches for athletes, they worked on a small retainer; getting paid only if their athletes achieved the results they had contracted for—up ticks in world ranking, for example, or a world championship. Accordingly, Jim and Jack were uninterested in pop-psychology and feel-good philosophy. They focused on scientific training that produced tangible results. End of story.

And what results did they achieve? For starters, they had trained sixteen athletes who had ascended to the number-one world ranking in their sport.

Their corporate client list was equally sensational, especially given their relatively small size. Corporate clients included Steve Reinemund, who as CEO of PepsiCo led them to exceed Coca-Cola in market value for the first time in their history; Peter Scaturro, then CEO of Citibank's private banking division; Phebe Farrow Port, executive with The Estée Lauder Companies, and many more. What also excited us was that most of their clients weren't Human Resource people but senior line leaders, and not infrequently CEOs. This is very unusual in the training and development industry, so we were intrigued.

The Human Performance Institute in general, and Jim Loehr and Jack Groppel in particular, impressed us deeply. But what was their message, the unique value proposition that captured the attention of some of the country's top executives? And why did their message— once you left the workshop and applied it—appear to actually stick? Although I knew a bit about their *Energy Management Technology*, I had to learn more.

Many of the principles I learned are expressed eloquently in Part I of this book. As I became acquainted with these tenets, they were compelling to me: They seemed so simple, accessible and intuitive. A few points especially resonated with me:

- ❑ Energy, not time, is the fundamental currency of high performance. It's not the amount of time one invests in a project that drives success but rather the energy one brings to the time he or she has. Time has value only in its intersection with energy.

- ❑ Deepening employee engagement is essentially an energy management challenge. Managing energy, managing engagement and managing effort are

functionally equivalent.
- ❑ Learning to manage energy is an acquired skill set that can be enhanced through training in much the same way that skills for managing time and money can be cultivated.
- ❑ Human energy and engagement are not single-faceted; rather, they are multidimensional in scope. By learning to manage the physical, emotional, mental and spiritual aspects of energy more efficiently and effectively, employees' performance, health and happiness can be significantly enhanced.

These ideas were profound, grounded in solid science and had a strong common sense appeal. In the end, I came to see that HPI's most important promise, its unique value proposition, was simple, attainable and compelling: If employees learn to more skillfully manage their energy, the full realization of their talent and skill becomes tangible.

You can probably see where this is going. My due diligence on the Human Performance Institute revealed a company that not only impressed me, but which I was passionate to join. When I was offered the presidency, I was elated. Just months before, I couldn't have imagined uprooting my family from the West (I grew up in California), but now we were off on our journey.

In the five years I have now been with HPI, Jim, Jack and our team have expanded and refined our offerings, so that senior line leaders—including numerous CEOs—at many of the world's biggest and most respected corporations have come through our programs. Perhaps more importantly, we have taken what has been an elite curriculum for a select few and democratized our training so it can be delivered to all levels of the organizations we serve. Some of these businesses include: Procter & Gamble. GlaxoSmithKline. PepsiCo. Allstate Insurance. Dell. Citi. Nordstrom. Microsoft. Additionally, we have worked with some small-to-medium sized businesses like The Breakers in Palm Beach, Florida (approximately 2,000 employees) and the San Juan Regional Medical Center (SJRMC) in Farmington, New Mexico (around 1,400 employees). The list goes on. The primary initiatives we work on with them include:

❑ *Productivity and Performance Initiatives.* We live in a global economy that begs us to compete at new levels and creates new time demands; we are wired up for nonstop productivity and the bar for performance is raised each year. These realities not only create relentless pressure to perform but also create a powerful case for developing the skills to expand our energy capacity and manage our energy more effectively. We can't expand time, but we *can* expand our energy capacity. The new skill of energy management can be learned and cultivated, and is a critical skill to meet the new demands of global competitive pressures and our 24/7 economy.

❑ *Great-Place-to-Work Initiatives.* Today, getting paid extremely well is not sufficient to recruit and retain top talent. In a post 9/11 economy, top talent demands a culture that respects people's needs both at work *and* outside of work. Our training helps individuals manage and focus their energy on what matters most in their professional and personal lives so that both can be fulfilling. Time management alone will not get this job done. Time, even when it is blocked out and given, brings nominal returns if you are burnt out and have negative energy. The key to a fulfilling life is not time but recruiting the correct quantity, quality, focus and force of energy when you need it most.

   We appreciate that employees' work lives, as well as their personal lives, are highly demanding. To get their lives to work effectively, employees must meet all demands. To meet all expectations, extraordinary energy reserves must be available whenever and wherever they are needed.

❑ *Health and Well-Being Initiatives.* According to the U.S. Centers for Disease Control and Prevention, nearly one out of every three adults (aged 20 to 74) is now considered obese and research shows that this population accounts for a substantial increase in the number of healthcare claims. Healthcare costs have sky-rocketed and the trends are not positive. (Obesity had risen from 15 percent of the population to over 32 percent between 1980 and 2004.)[1] Our corporate athlete training works on this problem by teaching proper nutrition and fitness and advocating them as keys to a more fulfilling life and to managing your energy more effectively.

When Procter & Gamble's CEO, A.G. Lafley, finished our executive course, he asked us how he could roll this program out to all of his employees—over 140,000 people. Since he wasn't about to send all 140,000 employees to Orlando for training, we created an intellectual property agreement with Procter & Gamble (P&G) that allows them to go global with this course in a very cost-effective way. They have now educated over 200 internal people to deliver the training to their employees. Amazingly, none of the people conducting the program are full-time trainers; they come from a variety of different functions and business roles.

One P&G story of significance surrounds the impact of the corporate athlete training on the Gillette's executive team. P&G acquired Gillette in October 2005 for US$57 billion, marrying two very strong companies in what billionaire Warren Buffett reportedly called a "dream deal," and who added, "This merger is going to create the greatest consumer products company in the world."[2] Both companies had outstanding results over the first half of the decade, and each had very strong, yet different, corporate cultures.

In October of 2006, A.G. asked Chip Bergh to lead the Gillette Blades & Razors business. Part of Chip's challenge was to integrate the business and the organization into Procter & Gamble, keeping as many of Gillette's best practices and best people, while at the same time keeping the business growth going during a period of great disruption that any merger brings. Chip's leadership team was a blend of outstanding Gillette executives and newly-added leaders from P&G. The immediate opportunity was to build a cohesive team with a common purpose and culture.

Chip was a "veteran" of the corporate athlete program, having been one of the first P&G employees to attend in 2004. He knew the profound impact it had on him personally but also on his previous organization when he was leading P&G's business in Asia. He chose the corporate athlete program as an intentional intervention to create a new, common culture, and a way to achieve breakthrough engagement with his leadership team through this shared experience.

Four months into his new assignment, Chip brought his global leadership team—a diverse blend of P&G and Gillette legacy talent from around the world—to Orlando for the program in January 2007. Following the two-and-a-half-day session, they held a two-day strategy meeting, scheduled to begin with a 1-hour discussion of their insights and learning from the training of the corporate athlete experience. This "debriefing" session was so powerful, though, and filled with so much emotion, that he couldn't—and wouldn't—shut it down; it lasted all afternoon and was a catalyst for bringing his global team together. Chip comments that the training had an immense impact on some people and on the group, and it brought the team together in ways not even imaginable at first, helping to create a new culture and language partially built around the program.

First, Chip and his leadership team returned a year later, and have committed to returning again for a third year in a row, making it part of the "drumbeat" of the business. This creates constancy of purpose and accountability within the leadership group on being fully engaged. Second, Chip and his team have now deployed the training deep into the organization, training over 500 managers and leaders around the world on the principles of the corporate athlete. Chip says he has seen the transformation the principles of the corporate athlete have had not only on himself but on many of the people in his organization—people not only being fully engaged at work but leading happier and healthier lives in every aspect of their lives (C. Bergh, personal communication, April 30, 2008). So strong is his belief in the benefits of the program that he has attended three times, and even brought his two adult sons through on his own dime so they, too, could profit from our energy management technology.

At the Human Performance Institute, we have been fortunate to see how our training helps clients in strategic ways, but some organizations are even extending this training beyond—to family members and to the communities they serve. Steve Altmiller, CEO of the San

Juan Regional Medical Center (SJRMC), and several members of his management team went through the program, brought it back to their people, and observed across-the-board improvements at the hospital. In an interview with *Fortune Magazine*, "[Altmiller] credits [the training] with helping to retain employees. A more energized workforce, he notes, is also less likely to make mistakes. And he has noticed an increase in morale: 'At least once a week I have an employee thanking me for it.'"[3] But there is more. They made it their business to proactively impact the health and well-being of the community that SJRMC serves, and HPI is now joint-venturing with them to deliver our training to the three school districts they support.

Our strategic approach has also caught the attention of those who study business. Jack Groppel is an Adjunct Professor of Management at Northwestern's Kellogg School of Management and has been teaching energy management principles in their Executive MBA Program for years. After the Dean and several professors from the Ross School of Business at the University of Michigan completed our program, they partnered with HPI to train their incoming MBA students. Yes—all 300+!

Do we think our energy management technology can improve *anyone's* performance? Well, without meaning to sound cavalier: just about. After all, the U.S. Special Forces teams receive some of the finest leadership training in the world and already employ a comprehensive body-mind-heart-spirit approach. As you will see in Rear Admiral Ray Smith's story, the military, including Navy SEALs, have effectively applied our principles for their benefit; principles concerning the need to draw on all four energy dimensions, on energy expenditure and recovery, on stress exposure and on following positive rituals. They called upon these principles after they were deployed overseas, and it helped them to better execute their life-and-death missions and to navigate unexpected "storms."

Our corporate clients have effectively applied our technology to enhance their engagement no matter what definition "reality" takes on. In 2005, Eugene O'Kelly, then Chairman and CEO of KPMG, hired us to help them with their great-place-to-work initiative. He knew that KPMG partners endured significant professional and personal demands, and he was committed to finding ways to help them deal more effectively with these challenges. Gene and his board also knew that doing so was strategically crucial for their recruiting and retaining of talent. What Gene didn't know was that a malignant and inoperable brain tumor would soon be discovered and take his life in just a few short months. We had been working with him, his executive team and all their partners for more than a year when he learned that he had approximately 100 days to live.

Suddenly, at age 53, Gene had to deal with the biggest and last fight of his life. Stripped of the many years he had assumed he still had, he found profound value in the ideas underlying HPI's technology of energy management and full engagement. Of particular value was the contention that managing energy can make whatever time we have priceless. Gene shared his insights about his final days in his book, *Chasing Daylight*:[4] "In my opinion, and that of many others, the most important note [Jim Loehr] sounded was that we would have greater success in achieving our goals if we tried not so much to control time—an impossibility, as it is outside us—and instead tried to control energy—eminently possible, as it is within us."[4] Later he says, "I had always been a great believer in commitment, in every aspect of life that mattered to me...Unfortunately, though, commitment, particularly in the business world, had come to equal time. Too often, your commitment was routinely measured by how many hours you were willing to work. By how much time you would take from your family...If you gave away huge amounts of your time, then it followed that you had exhibited commitment. If you did not give so much time, then by definition your level of commitment was suspect. Time alone was the bellwether."[4]

How many of us are guilty of using time as the measure of commitment? How meaningful will our lives really be if we use this as the key metric? Is energy perhaps a more substantial metric? "It's *not* about time," writes Gene, "Commitment is about depth. It's about effort. It's about passion...Of course time is involved; it would be naïve and illogical to suggest otherwise. But commitment is best measured not by the *time* one is willing to *give up* but, more accurately, by the *energy* one wants to *put in*..."[4]

As Jim Loehr and Jack Groppel showed for years as successful advisors to athletes, it's all about results. At HPI, we measure lots of things—hardly surprising, given Jim and Jack's respective backgrounds in performance psychology, physiology and biomechanics.

But not everything can be measured—there are many unknown and unknowable numbers. For example, what is the monetary value of a happy client? While happy clients refer business, it is difficult to know precisely just how significant a return our happy client brings; but we *do* know that it is significant. Also, anyone familiar with research in human performance knows that it's very tough to isolate all the variables of performance.

In light of this, we are quite satisfied to leave the final judgment to our clients. We appreciate that people may feel transformed when they complete our two-and-a-half-day training. But does the methodology stick? A six-month follow-up of P&G employees who completed the training showed that 80 percent "had some specific, measurable improvement in their lives."[3] Their numbers and words, not ours. GlaxoSmithKline (GSK) has also done long-term studies of the impact of our training on their employees and the results mirrored those of Procter & Gamble.

In my years in training and development, and especially in my last five years with the Human Performance Institute, I have met many CEOs including numerous ones of multi-billion dollar firms. Interestingly, even the most successful of them confess to us that learning to manage their energy is a new skill, a skill at which they are—despite their considerable leadership ability—decidedly mediocre, or worse. These leaders have also acknowledged to us that once they learned to master this skill, they saw how surprisingly powerful it could be for them and for their organizations.

Perhaps this *was*, in fact, as Will Marre originally suggested, the "next big thing" in the field of human performance. Yet of far greater interest to the reader than Will's or my appraisal may be a third party perspective. *Fortune Magazine* featured a series entitled "Secrets of Greatness: How I Work," for which they interviewed many of our nation's greatest leaders. Among them? A.G. Lafley. Dubbed by *Fortune* as "the king of management," what did this esteemed leader of industry have to say when asked what was his own secret of greatness? "I have learned to manage my energy. I used to just focus on managing my time."[5]

Energy management *is* an idea whose time has come.

PART I: PRINCIPLES

Chapter 1

The Corporate Athlete® Advantage: Managing Energy

by Dr. Jim Loehr

Theoretical models serve to organize and integrate diverse ideas, constructs and scientific findings. Since the early 1980's, I have been driven to find the best model for integrating all the diverse sciences supportive to human performance. The best model is the simplest model, as long as it captures all the essential elements and underlying dynamics. Great models bring order, harmony and predictability to complex ideas and known facts. After many years of study, I concluded that the best model for understanding and improving human performance would be one that conceptualized the human body as a fully integrated, multi-dimensional energy system. Doing so provides distinct and significant training advantages from ease of understanding to more precision and specificity in training objectives and routines. Our experience in applying this energy model both in the world of sport and business has been equivalent in terms of performance outcomes. This chapter is devoted to detailing the energy management fundamentals that have proven so valuable in sports to the arena of business.

Managing Energy 101

Energy is undoubtedly our most precious resource. Without energy, nothing is possible. Just as the sun's energy spawns life in plants, and plants spawn life in humans, we spawn life in whatever we give our energy to. Yet sadly, most of us pay little attention to responsibly managing this finite resource. I know what you may be thinking right now: "Wait, we have to *manage* our energy?" Though its necessity may not seem obvious at first, we are quite used to managing other things we value as important, like trying to master the management of our time and money. But we fail to apply the same logic and urgency to managing our energy, often because we have mystified it as some abstract, intangible construct that we think we have little control over. As a result, we consume energy with little or no regard for where it comes from or how it is produced. And when the demands of life require more energy, we simply expect our bodies will ante it up. If the additional energy isn't mobilized, we are perplexed and frustrated.

We may not think about the evolutionary perspective of humans on a daily basis, but evolution has not primed us in many ways for the extended lifespan that we now enjoy due to advances in medicine and technology. But physically speaking, our bodies are still expecting a stay on earth of roughly 45 to 50 years. Consequently, the human system reaches its maximum capacity for expending and recovering energy between 25 and 30 years of age.[1] Left to unfold naturally, functional energy capacity declines predictably with each passing year after approximately 30 until death. The better the human energy system is maintained, the better the chance it will have to meet the extraordinary demands we place on it, and the greater the volume of energy it will be capable of producing during its extended span of existence.

Another factor is crucial to understand: Rhythmicity is the most basic force of nature.[2] This applies to energy, too. The energy-producing capacity of the human system is best maintained when the system is intermittently turned fully on and fully off. The rhythmic oscillation of energy expenditure and recovery optimizes energy management. Extended intervals of work without recovery (in sports it's called *overtraining*) or extended intervals of recovery without work (i.e., *undertraining*) compromise energy production. In other words, without periodic renewal, the capacity of the system to expend energy eventually fails. This makes expending and recovering energy the most important functions in any living organism.

Growth follows energy investment. In order to grow the capacity of something, it must be exposed to stress. Stress means energy out, recovery means energy in. The rhythmic interaction of stress and re-covery creates the pulse of life. But as we can see, there is a delicate balance between stress and recovery. Training uses the principle of stress in a constructive way, helping to expand our system's capacity to produce energy. Training is effective at accomplishing this at almost any age. By repeating cycles of expending and recovering energy, we make our system more efficient; that is, by practicing stress-recovery-stress-recovery—a cyclic pattern that is in sync with the same oscilla-tion that governs life itself—we improve the strength, efficiency and capacity of our energy system.[3]

Energy Valences

The importance of *energy* as well as being attuned to how it func-tions in nature and in our bodies are very apparent now. But just as you cannot play a game well without knowing all of the rules, we cannot begin to make use of this basic knowledge without taking a closer look at and breaking down energy's DNA or composition. Clearly, human energy and effort is multi-dimensional—namely phys-ical, emotional, mental and spiritual.

To start, all human energy originates in the physical body and be-gins in the union of glucose and oxygen. Without sufficient physical energy, you can't produce high-quality amounts of three other kinds of important energy—emotional, mental and spiritual energy—mak-ing physical energy the cornerstone of energy management. Defin-ing these other dimensions as we interpret them will help aid you as you discover the benefits of the corporate athlete solution.

Emotional energy: The energy associated with feelings ranging from joy and challenge to anger and fear. Low physical energy com-promises our ability to give our best effort emotionally, something we refer to as emotional engagement, everywhere in our lives: We are less patient, less empathetic, less resilient—all in all more nega-tive.

Mental energy: The energy associated with cognitive processes such as thinking, analyzing and decision-making. Again, low physical energy reduces our daily ability to give our best effort mentally—

to engage mentally: Our concentration and memory are poorer, our thoughts more scattered, our perception of the world less objective and our rationale for actions become irrational. Regardless of how hard we try, low physical energy will repeatedly undermine our ability to achieve full mental engagement.

Spiritual energy: Physical energy also has a dynamic impact on our spiritual energy: the energy associated with purpose, values and beliefs. This energy manifests itself in our personal ethics, the passion we display for what we do and in our commitment. Essentially, spiritual energy is the energy of purpose. Additionally, clearly, low physical energy can erode our passion and commitment—even our very sense of purpose—toward what we are doing. In short, lack of physical energy undercuts pretty much everything we hold dear, in spite of our best efforts.

Energy Pyramid

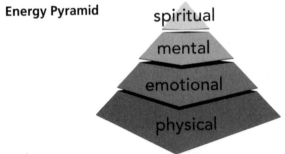

Figure 1

As depicted by the energy pyramid, you can see that it goes, in ascending order, from foundational to significant. The physical dimension is the foundation of who we are; and as we go up the triangle, the dimensions become more significant. These dimensions are interdependent, influencing each other all the time. Many training programs carve out sections of this model to enhance performance—a focus on emotional intelligence, for example, or on how to sharpen your mental skills to do your job better, or exploring the role of personal ethics in leadership. The corporate athlete model is among the first to look at performance improvement from a comprehensive, multidimensional perspective. Our unique hallmark, of course, is that we at the Human Performance Institute treat the physical body as critically important to business success.

Let's reiterate further the important concept that *growth follows energy investment.* Whatever receives our energy gains strength, for better or worse. Since every one of our thoughts, feelings and actions require energy, it stands that those that get more energy thrive, while those that get less or no energy wither or die. For example, the more energy we invest in anger, frustration, impatience or cynicism, the more powerful and dominant those traits become in us. Same for an investment of energy in hope, integrity, character, compassion and confidence. Growth ceases when energy investment ceases. Just as cutting off energy to a muscle causes atrophy, diverting energy away from impatience, negativity and helplessness causes them to atrophy.

Measuring Human Energy

The more you know of a construct's architecture such as energy, the better you can conceptually work with it. But you also need something else. You need a gauge for tracking progress along these dimensions or valences. Of course, if a resource can't be measured, then it can't be managed. If time or money couldn't be measured, then attempts to manage them would be futile. Indeed, human energy, and likewise, engagement in something, can be accurately measured. Like all energy, human energy possesses quantity, quality, focus and force (intensity).

Quantity: The amount of fuel currently available for investment (at HPI we measure on a scale of 1 to 4, from physically tired to physically energized); this corresponds to the level of physical energy.

Quality: Whether the energy flows principally from opportunity-based positive emotions such as challenge or the sense of adventure, or from survival-based negative emotions such as anger or fear. Positive emotions produce the highest quality of energy (on a scale of 1 to 4, from negative to positive energy); this measure is associated with emotional energy.

Focus: Whether the energy is scattered (multitasking) or laser-like, focused on the here and now. Focused energy is a critical component to full engagement (1 to 4, from scattered to fully focused). It is a descriptor for mental energy.

Force: The intensity of the invested energy in alignment with purpose (1 to 4, from uncommitted to totally committed); this calculates the spiritual level of energy.

The greatest engagement occurs when the quantity, quality, focus and force of effort are maximized (Sweet Sixteen: 4 x 4 = 16). The intersection of energy intensity with energy quality provides important insight into the dynamics of human effort, the concept that opened this chapter. As seen in *Figure 2* below, four distinct cells of energy are represented: high negative, high positive, low negative and low positive. High negative is survival-based energy, highly toxic and represents a wide range of low-quality negative emotions such as anger, fear, distrust, frustration and anxiety. High positive is opportunity-based energy and represents a wide range of high-quality positive emotions such as challenge, sense of adventure, hope, fun and optimism, and is the cell of full engagement. Low negative is also survival-based energy and represents a form of forced recovery. Typical feelings are extreme fatigue, burnout, depression, complete loss of drive or motivation. Low positive energy is the cell of voluntary recovery. It is physical, emotional, mental and spiritual renewal, and most often experienced in the context of *strategic disengagement*. The more time one spends in high negative, the greater the volume of renewal and recovery (low positive) that will be required for sustaining energy balance. High positive is the energy of high performance.

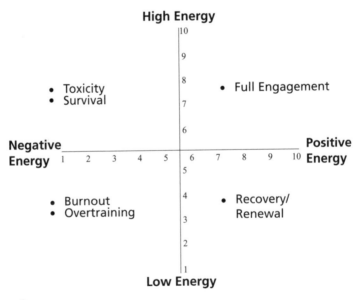

Figure 2

Understanding Engagement

The acquired ability to intentionally invest our full and best energy and effort in whatever we are doing at the moment (across all four dimensions) is what we refer to as *Full Engagement*. Full engagement requires the conscious recruitment of all dimensions of energy—physical, emotional, mental and spiritual. It represents the greatest quantity, highest quality, most precise focus and greatest intensity of effort invested in whatever we are doing at the time. Engagement never occurs in the future or in the past. It occurs right here, right now or it doesn't occur at all. Engagement and the present moment are inseparable.

This exposes a major deficiency in the promise of time management—the industry that has been the guiding principle for most in the corporate world and for personal enrichment, too. The reality is that time management simply takes us from being absent to being present. (Human Resource professionals call this unengaged condition "presenteeism.")[4] We are never late for appointments and always there for meetings. But being present in no way guarantees that we are really "there." Though time may be a prerequisite for energy investment, time only gains value in its intersection with energy. Investing time without energy produces nothing.

Another concept that has been encouraged by most organizations is multitasking.[5] Multitasking is the antithesis of full engagement—the enemy of extraordinary. Multitasking is defined as working on two or more unrelated tasks simultaneously. Examples would include talking on a cell phone while driving or working on a laptop computer while attending a meeting that has nothing to do with the laptop activity. Unfortunately for us, here is another example where evolution has not yet conditioned us for the complex world we live in as the human energy system is binary. No evidence currently exists that indicates human beings can focus on two or more parallel tasks simultaneously. The energy signal cannot be split. Or, more simply, there is either focus or no focus. The consequences of such a dichotomy? It has been shown that multitasking significantly increases the risk of error or accident on the job. It gives credence to the following imperative: Fully engage when the outcome is important and only multitask when it isn't.

We can see that engagement is, to say the least, very important. It is the gateway to real results, to immersion in activities and to intimacy in relationships; and because engagement spawns growth and full engagement spawns extraordinary growth, engagement is the connecting factor that bridges us from ordinary to extraordinary. Engagement and its impact not only directly benefit us, they also represent the supreme gift human beings have to offer because, in a real sense, the gift of energy is the gift of life.

Attaining this state of full engagement, though, is not achieved in a vacuum. Rather, we must traverse through the constant threat or presence of formidable obstacles. The greatest barrier to *physical engagement* is fatigue; the one to *emotional engagement* is the presence of survival-based emotions such as fear or anger; the biggest hurdle to *mental engagement* is multitasking and faulty storytelling; and the one to *spiritual engagement* is unclear purpose.

In addition to the challenges along each dimension for activating full engagement, the human energy system overall is designed to conserve energy at all costs—to exact the lowest metabolic cost possible for any action (i.e., conserving energy is survival-based). Full engagement, however, requires extraordinary energy expenditure for opportunity-based achievement and therefore represents a unique and distinctive energy management challenge. We will see that tapping into the rhythm of oscillation will aid in managing our energy, and in turn, being fully engaged. The next section discusses different natural cycles that we must be attuned to in order to harness our energy and optimize energy management.

Energy Expenditure and Recovery: Training for Full Engagement®

Training represents an integral part of reaching full engagement, because, as noted earlier, our natural capacity for energy production declines with age. Looking at the big picture, cycles of full engagement are best sustained with brief intervals of recovery (5 to 15 minutes) approximately every 90 minutes.[6] The more fit one is physically, emotionally, mentally and spiritually, the shorter the required interval of recovery required to sustain energy output.

But, as we now should be familiar, we must work with the individual components of energy in order to have all of our cylinders operating in harmony. The greater the volume of stored energy, the greater the quantity of energy that can be expended. In other words, the greater the skill in optimizing recovery, the greater the volume of work that can ultimately be done.

The primary mechanisms for physical recovery are nutritional intake, hydration, respiratory fitness (oxygen transport efficiency), and periodic oscillation between movement and non-movement. Recovery emotionally, mentally and spiritually occurs by turning off (disengaging) from whatever is causing energy to be expended in a particular dimension. For example, going for a run, which is a form of physical stress, may double as a valuable form of emotional and mental recovery as long as the act of running allows the person to disengage from those things that resulted in energy expenditure in the other dimensions.

The following constitute some of the basic cycles to which we— as energy systems—are bound, and thus must be abided by in order to maintain optimal operational efficiency (and prerequisites for full engagement). As they will be further explained in the next two chapters on nutrition and movement, I mention them only briefly in the context of an enumeration of oscillations within our energy systems that impact our ability to fully engage.

❑ The human energy system must be turned off (in sleep mode) approximately one-third of every 24 hours. Most individuals require 7 to 8 hours of sleep daily. However, highly fit individuals require less: This acknowledges the idea that speed of recovery is an important measure of fitness. Furthermore, going to bed early and waking up early, and going to bed and getting up at consistently the same time, allow for high-quality energy production through ritualized recovery.

❑ During waking hours, another cycle, pertaining to movement and non-movement, continues to help us optimize engagement. To prevent mental and emotional disengagement when the muscular system is idle (no movement) for prolonged periods, small movements of the hands, feet and arms should be made every 30 to 40 minutes, and large movements such as walking, climbing stairs or full body stretching should be practiced every 90 to 120 minutes. This is crucial as movement facilitates oxygen transport to the cells.

❏ As energy originates in the union of oxygen and glucose, glucose, too, has a corresponding cycle for maximum energy efficiency: It must be added to the system every 3 to 4 hours at a minimum. The only exception is during the 7 to 8 hours of nighttime sleep. Anything that destabilizes blood glucose levels effectively destabilizes energy production and engagement. Nutritional practices that stabilize blood glucose would thus be advantageous, and include eating often and light, eating breakfast every day, consuming low-glycemic foods and eating until one is satisfied, not full. Of course, it is optimal when water is added every 30 to 60 minutes for the functioning of the human's energy system.

❏ One final cycle that facilitates the maintenance of the human energy system regards daily physical activity. (This is different than the small and large periodic movements previously mentioned.) A minimum of two cardiovascular interval workouts a week are required for maintaining full cardiovascular energy output, and two strength training sessions per week are required for maintaining optimal muscle capacity (the ability to exert and resist force).

These cycles, whether we are aware of them or not, and whether we try to work with them or not, govern our energy systems. It would be of our greatest interest to attune ourselves to them in order to maximize our best energy right here, right now. It is through full engagement that we move from ordinary to extraordinary.

From Chaos to Order

Human beings are complex energy systems. Each of us represents a cell of potential energy that can be mobilized in the service of any cause or mission, corporate or otherwise. The more energy we have, the greater the volume of work we can do, and in turn, the greater the potential impact we can have in the world.

All energy systems naturally move toward chaos and disorder— its scientific term is entropy—and the human energy system is no exception.[7] (Remember that great achievement does not and cannot realistically occur in a vacuum.) So how is it that we can sustain the course toward a goal with entropy constantly trying to undermine the mobilization of energy? The answer: The ordering force in human energy is purpose. Purpose orders and directs human energy. Human beings function best when expending energy in the service of something deeply meaningful to them. We are clearly a mission-specific species. In essence, purpose gives us a structure around which to harness energy. Thus, the energy system works best within the context of a clearly defined, meaningful mission; it becomes inefficient and chaotic in the absence of a meaningful mission.

In spite of the fact that full engagement is a conscious, intentional act, it occurs not by will power or self-discipline but by habit and routine. In fact, as much as 95 percent of human behavior is under the control of habit.[8] Consequently, anything new that we seek to accomplish must tap into conscious effort. The consciously acquired habits that enhance efficient energy management are called rituals. Rituals ensure that one habitually and skillfully manages energy in support of a targeted mission.

Organizational Energy

Organizations, too, are complex energy systems: They represent a collection of all the individual cells of potential energy (their workforce). So the more energy individual team members possess, the greater the volume of work that can potentially be accomplished on behalf of the organization. And like human beings, organizations have a physical as well as an emotional, mental and spiritual pulse. The stronger the pulse, the greater the capacity for work, and the greater the capacity for producing extraordinary outcomes. Strengthening the individuals' and organization's pulse is thus a primary objective of energy management training.

All *organizational energy* (the pulse) originates in the physical bodies of employees. Again, physical energy is the limiting factor in the equation for full engagement: The other dimensions can only exist proportional to the reservoir of physical energy. Thus, if there is a shortage of physical energy, the other dimensions cannot expand beyond the limits of that shortage. Organizationally speaking, without physical energy, organizational productivity ceases.

Also like individuals, organizational health is reflected in the functional ability to expend and recover energy efficiently. The healthier individuals or organizations are, the more energy they typically have for investment. But diseases eventually compromise energy production.

Leaders lead most importantly with their energy. Fundamentally, leadership is mobilizing, focusing and renewing energy in the service of the agreed upon mission. Energy is highly contagious, both positive and negative. Some individuals are energizers and some are de-energizers. Some clearly stimulate energy in others, while some are so needy emotionally, mentally or spiritually, they can quickly exhaust the energy reserves of those around them. Emotional fragility, insecurity, defensiveness, hopelessness or lack of vision may require what seem to be endless energy investments to keep some people functioning effectively in support of a mission. Compared to de-energizers, energizers are more productive, stimulate higher levels of productivity in others and tend to attract other energizers to their respective team. An important part of leadership is converting de-energizers into energizers.

If leaders can do so, individual's engagement will likely increase. Researchers have confirmed a strong link exists between engagement and issues of worker productivity, worker happiness and worker health. As engagement levels increase for employees, so also do their reported levels of productivity, perceived happiness and general physical health.

Energy Management and Storytelling

An important aspect of energy management in the mental dimension, both individually and organizationally, is storytelling. A story is simply a pathway for energy to flow neurologically. Stories ensure that certain thoughts, feelings and beliefs get consistently nourished and are kept alive while others are allowed to die from lack of energy investment. Everything we say is a story. We live our lives through stories. The only reality we know is the one we create with our stories. We literally become the architects of our own reality through our storytelling. Some stories engage and inspire; others disengage and spawn helplessness and defeat (similar to energizers and de-energizers). Great leaders manage energy through the stories they tell themselves and others. The stories of great leaders are grounded in truth, are purpose-driven and inspire hope-filled action in those they are leading. In reality, stories drive destiny, both individually and organizationally.

Every story that exists in people's lives has an assigned area of neurological real estate that corresponds to it, called a neuro-network.[9] Large-scale change in an individual's story requires change in the neuro-network, which in turn changes the way energy flows. The brain can, in fact, change its neuro-network in response to repeated energy investments. Thus, conscious investment of energy over time in dynamics such as compassion, kindness, patience or gratitude causes them to functionally expand.[10, 11] Repetitious energy expenditure in a specific direction results in chemical and physical changes in the brain's operating structure. Intentional investment of energy changes neurological architecture.

Energy density represents the total volume of energy (effort) invested in a specific direction—that is, where our stories take us. The greater the energy density, the greater the potential for change. And we change the future by changing the way we invest energy in the present.

Conclusion

All sport training is fundamentally grounded in the application of energy management skills. Becoming an elite athlete and managing energy and effort are nearly synonymous. Issues of training tables, fitness, attitude, goal setting, intensity, concentration, training logs and motivation are all dynamically connected within the framework of managing energy. The world of sport, particularly professional sport, is driven by tangible numbers and measurable outcomes just like business. The energy management lessons acquired from professional sport apply directly to the world of high performance in most any arena. Once it is acknowledged that the fundamental currency of performance, like professional sport, is energy and that all business functions depend on human energy for execution, creating corporate cultures supportive to skillful energy management becomes both strategic and imperative. Rarely does energy management warrant serious consideration in the design of corporate leadership programs. Inspiration, motivation, persistence, resiliency, passion and even sound and ethical decision-making are fundamentally energy based. Fatigue undermines all business functions in the same way loss of power prevents software accessibility in computer systems. The software, however brilliant, remains dormant until the power supply and operating system are properly functioning. In human beings, the body is the power supply and operating system. Disconnecting software functions from their power supply and operating systems in the management of computer systems would be unthinkable in business. But that's exactly what happens when the human body is carved out of the formula of high performance. By saying that the software between a performer's ears is relevant but the power supply and operating systems (the body) are not, a tragic disconnect is set in motion.

Maximizing worker productivity and engagement brings leaders face to face with the energy management technology briefly outlined in this chapter. Human beings are multi-dimensional, fully integrated energy systems; and businesses that truly embrace the holistic design of the human energy system in their training and leadership programs will experience unprecedented levels of employee engagement, loyalty, retention and productivity over time. Training employees to manage energy and effort as skillfully as Olympians and providing the support, encouragement and education to do so in the work environment, is an exciting new direction for many organizations. More than 30 years of experience in high-stress, mission-critical venues, has driven home two simple but profound truths:

1. High performance, improved health and greater happiness happen when—and only when—employees manage their energy well.
2. The most direct path for increasing employee productivity and engagement involves managing energy, not just time.

Chapter 2

Stories About Food: Those that Nourish, Those that Don't

by Raquel Malo

Food is energy.

For better or worse.

The number of people arriving at our workshop that don't really understand the connection between food intake and energy production is amazing. Oh, sure, they understand on an intellectual level that energy comes from the breakdown of food in the body, and that the more nutritious the food, the better it is for you, in general. But then these incredibly intelligent executives are just shocked—shocked!—when we insist that, yes, the only way for them to get their best *energy*, and to perform consistently at their peak, is by eating certain types of food in certain quantities at certain intervals (among other strategic habits). When they arrive at the Human Performance Institute, these tremendously successful businesswomen and men appreciate—and in the same breath disregard—that the reason they turn moody or irritable or get headaches or have trouble listening well or staying awake during the day could be primarily, if not exclusively, a function of their food intake. A headache? Take an aspirin. Moodiness? Maybe another sweet. They treat the symptom but don't acknowledge the healthier, more fundamental way to fix the source of these symptoms.

The effect of food on the human energy system is profound. Poor nutrition unquestionably affects your physical energy, and thus (as discussed in *Chapter 1*) your emotional, mental and spiritual energy. Admittedly, that's a grand claim. What does it mean to say that improper nutrition affects your spiritual energy? It means that because you ate poorly at your last meal, your very sense of purpose is negatively affected; what you ate has compromised your perception of who you are as a person (not to mention "lesser" aspects of your behavior and functioning like mood and decision-making ability). To show how profoundly true "food is energy" really is: If you don't eat correctly, you can't align your energy with your sense of purpose because the energy won't be there. You cannot be the person you want to be. On the other hand, if you do eat correctly, then you are more likely to be that person and live a higher quality life.

So why is it that the inverse of that truth—namely, if you care about living a quality life, then you will eat correctly—is practiced by so few of the brilliant folks we work with?

It's hard to say. As I said, they understand, at least theoretically, the truth of "food is energy" (which, by the way, is the abridged version that, when expanded, includes "how much food" and also "what kind of food" and "when"). For many of our clients, though, it's just a slogan. Its message doesn't apply to them. They will tell you they don't have time to eat better. Or that they lack the flexibility of schedule to eat when they should. Or that when food *is* available they don't necessarily need it, but it makes sense to partake (i.e., overfuel) anyway. Or that it's just too hard to eat less in many situations. Or that it's impossible to stop for a much needed snack at some inopportune moment. To them these represent adequate explanations for their less than stellar eating habits. To us they are lousy stories about nutrition.

There are numerous valid reasons why people eat poorly: Today's culture does not properly value good nutrition and fresh, whole foods; people are so genuinely busy that there is insufficient time to prepare well-balanced, home-cooked meals on a regular basis; so much of our environment and culture provides huge portions of food and snacks tempting us to eat it all. And there are many other seemingly legitimate reasons.

While I acknowledge that today's work-life is hectic with many apparent obstacles to strategic eating, these obstacles are not insurmountable. Yet they *seem* so because we have become very good at telling ourselves stories to convince ourselves to discount our actions.

That's all they are: stories. Not facts. Not truths. Just stories about food and eating that we tell ourselves enough times that eventually they "appear" true to us. And we hope others in turn will believe them to be true.

I want to spend the majority of this chapter on *storytelling*—what our current food stories proclaim, why they ultimately fail us, and how we need new, constructive, *truthful* stories about food. You will know a "new story" is true because, in following it, you will eat strategically and consistently, thus positioning yourself to live the most energetic, productive, fulfilled, balanced, healthy life possible.

First, though, a few basics to good eating:

- ❏ Your body depends on glucose. To manage your energy means, in large part, to manage your glucose. Anything that destabilizes blood glucose level destabilizes energy production. While other factors influence the glucose level (i.e., how much you exert yourself or external conditions), food has the largest impact.

- ❏ To keep your energy level up and consistent—and to avoid those peaks and valleys so familiar during the workday—glucose must be added to the system every 3 to 4 hours, at minimum. The lone exception is the 7- to 8-hour stretch of nighttime sleep. Examples of nutritional practices that stabilize blood glucose are eating often and light, eating breakfast every day, consuming low-glycemic snacks and eating until one is satisfied, not full.

- ❏ Our energy system functions best when we add water to it every 30 to 60 minutes.

- ❏ A meal must consist of a balance between protein and carbohydrates.

There are more basics (i.e., eat a variety of foods or eat slowly), but for the time being I think the preceding rules cover the fundamental truths—namely, appreciate and understand how food affects energy; eat balanced meals; don't overeat; keep hydrated. By now you have probably already heard most of the rules about good eating more times than you care to count. In our workshops, our nutritional team and I cover these basics with our clients but soon shift our attention to what is discussed far less, and what may influence our eating decisions far more—the stories we tell about food. These are the reasons we start eating poorly.

From the time we are very young, people, especially our parents, tell us all kinds of stories about food. But these stories don't start the moment we are born, for two reasons: (1) We obviously wouldn't understand them; and (2) even if we could understand them, we would never heed them. Infants and very young children have no story about food. They eat when they are hungry. They don't eat when they are not hungry. End of story.

When children are old enough to understand, the stories begin, because parents can get very obsessive about food and their children. Mom wants her child always to eat just three more bites. Or Dad plays the "airplane" or "choo-choo train" game, figuring he must get more food into his child's belly. Children instinctively believe their parents know better how much food they need, which in turn teaches them to not trust signals from their own bodies about feeling full or not.

But these stories go beyond being about how much food the child eats. For example, perhaps the parents get their children to eat by pointing out that children in other countries are starving, therefore it's a sin to throw food away. So now a story has begun to develop in the child's mind that says, "If I don't eat, other children suffer."

Before it sounds like I am blaming parents for all faulty stories about food, it should be noted that many stories are generated early on by us. For example, younger siblings, especially ones from big families, may grow up in an atmosphere where they are always fighting for food, so he or she starts to feel, "If I don't eat it right now, then it won't be available later." That is a story that could stay with you for quite a while, even long after its "truth" is obsolete. There are creative stories about eating that develop in response to all kinds of problems at home. The possible sources for our stories (not just about food, of course, but about anything) are too numerous to list.

All these stories make some kind of sense. So they stay with us as we morph into adults and, one day, we awaken to the reality that some of these stories have had tragic consequences in our lives.

The problem is, stories are so powerful that they can alter our physical responses, and ultimately affect our health. If you don't believe that stories and psychology have the ability to affect physical behavior, why don't you get up and go to the restroom in the middle of a business meeting? Because long ago you figured out it would be frowned upon to leave the meeting at a crucial juncture, so you adapted. Stories can be devilishly hard to undo. And stories about something as elemental as eating may be particularly hard.

If you are going to perform and live your life the way you want, you must identify the potentially damaging stories you tell, particularly when those stories have such a direct effect on your physical energy level. Only by first identifying these stories can you start to change them. Fortunately—as we have seen numerous times—even extremely entrenched stories about eating can be replaced with positive ones.

The subsequent list is by no means complete. It's just meant to point out a few of the faulty food stories we encounter. You may recognize some of them.

The "Overeating" Story

As already mentioned, too many people grow up to be members of the "clean plate club"—that is, as children they were admonished to eat every last bite, even when they were full, because of unseen starving children, or the expense of the food, or the time it took to prepare it, etc. Bad story.

Do you know how little it takes to gain or lose weight? Many adults gain, on average, about a pound of fat a year; each pound has 3,500 calories; that works out to be ten calories of food per day, which is basically one bite of food per day. If you took one less bite a day, you would not gain that pound (all other things being equal). In essence, three fewer bites per day equates to three fewer pounds per year.

In reality, it doesn't work out exactly like that (all other things are never equal, of course), but my point is this: *No bite is a freebie.* To tell a small child, "Take just three more bites..." is a huge amount of food! Especially when the child is already satisfied! Children are better in tune with the amount of food they require for satiety because they have not developed stories yet. Stories often are corrosive and undermine our health, however, they don't have to be.

Today you find yourself eating more than you want at a restaurant because you paid for it. Or because food is just sitting there. Or because everyone else is finishing their meals. Start to change this bad habit or story this way: Develop the new habit of asking for a container to take home the portion of the meal you can't finish. In fact—strange as this may sound—ask for the container *when you order the meal*, not at the end. When the food and the container arrive, store the half you will be saving and put it away immediately, so that it's not visible during the entire meal, taunting you.

The "All I Need Is to Fuel My Tank Fast" Story

You are hungry. You eat. You are no longer hungry. You stop eating.

Wouldn't it be nice if it worked that simply, the way it does with infants? It rarely does with grown-ups. One of the main culprits is the speed with which we eat. Harried workers eat so quickly ("So much work, so little time...") that they cannot tell when they have reached their satiety level and continue to eat. There is a delay of about 15 to 20 minutes from the time food enters the system to the time the brain registers what has been consumed. The faster you inhale food, the more likely you are to lose all perception of what you actually acquired and require.

In fact, the act of chewing creates satisfaction; the more you chew, the more satisfied you feel. That's why I warn clients about consuming shakes as a way to fuel up: Shakes—power shakes, milk shakes, any kind of shake—are ultimately unsatisfying because you chew nothing; by the end, you have downed, say, 600 calories, and mostly feel bloated, not satisfied.

Add to this that many of us don't know anymore what it means to reach normal satisfaction after a meal—not full, not bloated, not on the verge of a food coma but simply satisfied. When you finish a meal, you should not feel food sitting in your stomach. Right after children eat, they go play, they rarely cramp or get sick. As adults, though, we have been trained to eat until we are full for a variety of reasons. This mindset, this story, has been reinforced so many times, we believe it is reality.

Here are some tips to deal with this bad story:

1. Slow down when eating. Take breaths between bites. Chew more. Put your fork or spoon down periodically. Remind yourself to taste what you are eating.
2. As soon as you start to feel *anything* in your stomach, stop eating.
3. For your next meal, try to eat half of what you would normally eat. Put the other half away for 30 minutes. See how you feel. I'll bet 30 minutes later you won't crave any of the food you put away. In many situations, like restaurants, celebrations, family meals and even snacks, most people eat roughly double what they actually need.

The "It Doesn't Matter When I Eat" Story

If I exercise on an empty stomach, I will burn even more fat...

Ever said that to yourself? It may make sense in some simplistic, calories in/calories out sort of way. However, what you are doing is jeopardizing not just your workout—but also your health. When you expend energy, especially extraordinary energy—such as during a physically taxing workout—you must come to it armed with sufficient, high-quality fuel. If your fuel reserves are depleted, it will be much harder, if not impossible, for you to engage fully in what you are doing, thus undermining much of the point of the activity. Insufficient fuel (food) means that, rather than burning fat when you are working out—your objective—you will end up burning muscle—what you absolutely do not want. To exercise is laudable and necessary for physical health; to try and do it on little or no fuel—as if some kind of bonus will accrue to you for doing it that way—is a counterproductive, even dangerous story.

Remember: Energy management is not just about giving yourself the proper amount of fuel but also about preparing for extraordinary energy expenditures (like exercise) with extraordinary energy reserves.

The "Three Meals a Day Is Sufficient" Story

People who follow this story have been taught to eat three square meals a day, with no interim snacking—because snacking ruins your appetite. There is a lot wrong with this story—especially the part about "ruining your appetite." What does that mean? In fact, there is no such thing as ruining your appetite.

Unfortunately, many people have the idea that food averages out during the day. That all you need to do is to make sure, at three major interludes during the day, to take in a certain amount of good stuff—nutrients, vitamins, minerals, protein, etc.—because that's the full complement that you require for one whole day's worth of energy expenditure.

Energy does not work this way. Energy cannot be stored and expanded like that. When you put energy into the system, there is about a 4-hour window for it to be used up. When you eat, you are influencing your energy reserve for the next 4 hours—not the next ten. If in the next 4 hours you don't expend that energy, it's not as if there is this available compartment for the extra fuel until you *do* need to spend the energy. Conversely, if your energy needs are great and your food intake in the previous 4 hours has not been sufficient, then you will begin to falter if you don't go ahead and get some more fuel.

So go ahead and ruin your appetite—or risk operating in a depleted way until your next meal (at which point you will be likely to binge, since you have been fuel-deprived for some time). Have you ever told yourself, "Gosh, we are having dinner so late today, I should eat a really big lunch now..."? That big lunch will put you in a food coma and will do nothing for you 6 hours later when you are pining for that dinner that is still a couple hours away.

The way to undo this story:

1. Snack, snack, snack. Snacks are not mini meals; they don't have to be as balanced as meals, because your meal already provided you with some of your nutrient needs. Perhaps a banana will give you the short-term energy boost you need; that may last an hour or so—at which point you should snack again. The whole system of "three square meals" is really a social con-

vention, and not particularly attuned to our energy requirements. The fact is, unless you are living a very low energy, even passive lifestyle, you will want—indeed, need—to supplement the fuel you obtain from meals with the fuel you get from snacks.

2. When you snack, beware the glycemic index (GI) of the foods you choose; you are looking for sustainable energy for the next short period of time. Some foods and food combinations are fine, and some are not. For a list of the best snacks and their GI, please refer to HPI's website: www.corporateathlete.com.

The "If I'm Not Eating Healthy, Then It Doesn't Matter How Unhealthily I'm Eating" Story (a.k.a. The "My Next Meal Is the First Meal of the Rest of My Life" Story)

Often the choices seem limited to takeout, or food that is not fresh, or a poor nutritional balance—you convince yourself you need fuel, you need it now, and you will take what is in front of you. Since today is clearly not the day you are able to eat healthy, then how much can it matter if you get the fried version, or the jumbo order... Unhealthy is unhealthy, right?

There is some obviously dubious math being allied here, yet so many people compute in this manner.

As I stated earlier: No bite is a freebie. Everything that goes in your mouth counts. If you overeat a little, it affects you a little; if you overeat a lot, it affects you a lot. Eating something that's really bad for you is worse than eating something that's only a little bad. So if your choices aren't ideal, you can still control what you eat and how much. Just because you don't control everything you would like to control, you still control some things.

(A subset of this might be called The *"At Least I'm Getting It Somehow" Story*: Many clients will point out that they do obtain enough protein from their diet—it just happens to be from fatty red meat, say; or they do consume enough grain—it just happens to come from beer; or they do hydrate enough—it just happens to be from juice, soda and coffee. This is yet another bad story. Take the hydration example: Yes, you are drinking "water," but those beverages are loaded with lots of other stuff that could interfere with nutrient absorption. Along with the water, you are also getting an excess of glucose, which is found in abundance in soda and juice, and which can contribute to obesity or diabetes. So in order to meet your daily nutrient needs without regard for how you acquired them is short-sighted and will not lead to quality energy.)

The "It Doesn't Matter if I Eat a Huge, Food-Coma-Inducing Dinner Since I'm Shutting Down for the Night Anyway" Story
What difference does it make, right?

The fact is, you should go to sleep neither hungry nor bloated. If you do the former, you will compromise energy and trigger muscle loss. (Just because you are sleeping doesn't mean you are not using energy.) If you do the latter, you will compromise energy, store fat and diminish the quality of your sleep.

As with other bad stories, changing this one is relatively simple, however, in this case requires the acceptance of an idea that many clients find difficult: snacking late at night, in the hours after dinner and before bedtime. Really. It's okay to snack at night. That doesn't mean 5 minutes before you plan to be asleep; it could be 45 minutes to an hour before. It's okay. Really. By not overeating at dinner, and by snacking judiciously the rest of the evening, you keep your blood sugar level more consistent, and you will obtain superior sleep.

As I said, the preceding catalogue of stories is only a sampling. There are many, many more. (Any candidates for *The "I just Ran Eight Miles so I Can Eat Whatever I Want the Rest of the Day" Story*?) With clients in our workshop, we ask them to identify their bad habits and evaluate the negative impact these habits contribute to their energy management. No bad stories affect energy management more than bad stories about food—the very fuel we need for physical energy.

It's vital that we learn from our infant selves to listen to our bodies. The mealtime cues that trigger us to eat as we get older—social acceptance, politeness, awareness of the cost of food, boredom, etc.—are pale reasons for feeding our bodies. The first and last reason should be to fuel ourselves well so that we can accomplish in our lives what we most want and need to. If we follow this story, then the *way* we fuel ourselves will be efficient, consistent and adequate; not wasteful, counterproductive or without purpose. We must return to a way that works. We must pay better attention to our stomach. When eating, we must stop and ask ourselves: "Have I overeaten? Am I full? Satisfied? Still hungry?" If your stomach growls from hunger within 2 hours of a meal, then you did not eat enough...something that almost never happens.

The uplifting news: By heeding your body, by being more strategic in snacking and making sure to obtain proper, nutritious fuel when you need it, you will realize the change almost immediately. It's no exaggeration to say that within one to three weeks of following your new story about food you will transform—no longer bloated, no longer dealing with those mid-morning, mid-afternoon energy peaks and valleys, no longer exhausted at the end of the day, no longer irritable, distracted, unengaged, unproductive, unfulfilled. If you couple your new story about food with an equally good one about exercise and recovery, you will, in remarkably short order, become leaner, lose weight and see improvement in other key health indices (blood pressure, cholesterol and triglyceride levels, etc.). You will not binge. When hungry, your body will crave more nutritious food. Your body will tell you when it needs more and when it has enough. Since you are re-learning, it will take practice. There will be trial and error when it comes to portion size, when to eat and what to eat. But if you listen carefully to your own body, you will be surprised at its accuracy. Like so many of the clients at the Human Performance Institute with whom I have been privileged to work, your new story about food can aptly be called only one thing:

A success story.

Chapter 3

Don't Just Sit There...
Move Something!
Movement, Exercise and Recovery for Maximum Energy and Performance

by Chris Jordan

These days, very few business professionals have what appear to be physically demanding jobs.

There. I said it. Sorry to point it out. And I understand it's not true of everyone. But it's predominantly true, certainly if our clientele at the Human Performance Institute is indicative. There are many sedentary activities: sitting at desks, computer work, attending meetings, talking on the phone (credit those who actually pick up the receiver versus always talking on speaker phone), attending more meetings, thinking, sitting, writing, reading, e-mailing, text messaging.

Please don't misunderstand, just because your job isn't physically demanding doesn't mean it's not demanding lots of mental and emotional energy, which no doubt it is. But physically demanding? Unlikely.

Or is it? The jobs of some of our clients—military units and law enforcement, say, and some medical professionals, not to mention the many professional athletes who come through our doors—are physically rigorous, no question. These professionals *know* they must have adequate physical energy when they arrive at work, or they simply won't be able to do their job well, if at all; they know they must maintain good energy during the day to continue to perform.

In reality, however, you are probably more like them than you realize. I contend that you cannot come close to excelling at your job, whatever it is—even if it requires sitting at a desk for 8 hours, with only brief forays for lunch, bathroom breaks and maybe a short stroll down the hall for the 11 a.m. meeting—unless you are physically prepared. I mean *genuinely* prepared. Think for a moment: When is your most productive time of day? It varies among individuals, but for many it is the morning. Typically, this highly productive stretch is characterized by alertness, focus, positive energy, a feeling that you are equal to any task, no matter how challenging. What is your physical energy level amid this productive time? High, of course.

Now think about the time of day when you are *least* productive. Again, it varies among individuals, however, there is one particular time when a great number of people become especially sluggish: early to mid-afternoon. At this time of day, many people are moody, impatient, irritable, and show decreased enthusiasm for and commitment to their work. They find it tough to remain focused on tasks. Sound familiar?

Or perhaps this scenario rings a bell: Your energy at work is fine. It's when you *leave* your office that the problem begins. Your energy is all spent. For the people who matter most to you—your family—you have little or no energy available.

As you have learned in *Chapter 1*, energy might usefully be seen as four-dimensional: physical, emotional, mental and spiritual. Physical energy is the basis for all energy; as such, it directly influences the other three dimensions. How do you feel *emotionally* after a particularly long day at work? Perhaps impatient or frustrated (from dealing with traffic), or less than sociable (not great if you are scheduled to meet friends), perhaps exhausted, even defeated. What happens *mentally* when you are fatigued from work, or after a poor night's sleep? You probably find it hard to concentrate, to focus on the tasks at hand, to solve the problems you need to solve. How do you feel *spiritually*? Perhaps you start to wonder why you waste so much of your time doing what you are doing, or you question your very career choice (along with many other major life choices).

All this turmoil really comes about merely because your tank of physical energy is low.

Perhaps this example from my own life will serve to illustrate how physical energy—the foundational energy, if you will—influences (a euphemism here for "corrupts") the other three dimensions of energy. I live in Orlando, Florida with my girlfriend. A few years ago, early in our relationship, I decided to surprise her with a trip to my native country, England, for the Holidays, to tour the country, meet my parents and spend the holiday with my family. She was ecstatic as she had never traveled to England, and was as thrilled at the prospect of meeting my parents as they were to finally meet her. Our flight was nonstop from Orlando to London. For most of the first hour, we held hands and she kept expressing how happy she was. After 2 hours, we stopped holding hands. After three, we stopped talking. By the time we landed in England, 8 hours later—plus losing 5 hours traveling across time zones—we were arguing about something so insignificant we didn't even know what it was. It felt as if our whole relationship was hanging by the proverbial thread.

The reason for all this agitation and misery? Physical fatigue. Our energy levels were so low after a night flight, where we were unable to sleep and had crossed five time zones, that we became moody and impatient (low emotional energy), irrational and unfocused (low mental energy), and suddenly didn't even care about the trip (low spiritual energy). I'm happy to report that, after a rest and some food (energy recovery), we recovered. The trip turned out to be a complete success.

Without question, physical fatigue seriously compromises our ability to be at our best in all dimensions. Conversely, being physically energized is a prerequisite for peak performance in all dimensions. To achieve peak performance, we absolutely must manage our energy wisely.

Smart energy management takes us where we want to go, while time management—what most people practice—takes us only from being absent to being present. It does not guarantee performance or productivity. I learned this when I began working as an exercise physiologist for the United States Air Force, my employer for almost seven years. In January 1997, I was charged with the fitness testing of 5,000 active-duty personnel at a base in England. Yes, it was as immense a task as it sounds, and I wasn't sure if it could be accomplished: I was the first exercise physiologist to take on this job at this base. The workload was a lot more than I had ever experienced. There didn't seem enough hours in the day. Time was precious and I struggled to learn how to manage my time effectively—or so I thought. Not long after, I had traded in my daily workouts and neglected breakfast and lunch to spend more time working. However, it made little, if any, impact on the total work I accomplished each day.

Then I started to notice how my supervisor operated. A U.S. Air Force Major, she was in charge of the Health and Wellness Center where I worked. I thought *my* responsibilities and workload were immense. They paled next to hers. Plus, she had a husband and two children. She worked tirelessly in spite of the knowledge that, at any moment, she could be sent on a mission halfway around the world. (As a non-American and non-military, I had no such obligation.) Yes, she had great time management skills, but she also had great energy management skills. No matter how busy her day, she always had her water bottle, and I could see her sipping from it often. Between breakfast and lunch, and between lunch and dinner, she would snack on fruit (or something with fruit) or some other healthy snack. I never saw her miss a day of exercise, no matter the circumstances. Either she would bike to work, exercise at lunchtime, run at the end of the day, or attend one of the workout classes on the base. Her energy seemed boundless. Here was a person who got things done and was respected by all who knew her. I began to understand that it was not enough just to manage my time. It was at least as important to manage my energy, too.

Ultimately, I was promoted to Fitness Program Consultant for the U.S. Air Force in Europe, this time overseeing the fitness testing of more than 30,000 active duty, a job that required many hours and an incredible amount of energy. I never could have accomplished everything had I not applied energy management.

The principles guiding my work with those tens of thousands of men and women (and for myself) are the same ones that guide the movement, exercise and recovery segment of our corporate athlete executive programs. What would a significant increase in physical energy do for you at work or at home? If I were able to almost instantly boost your daily levels of physical energy by 25 percent for the rest of your life, would that help you? Who besides you would benefit? What if I gave you the tools to better manage your energy? Wouldn't having more physical energy positively impact your productivity and performance? Let's look at how easily that can be obtained.

The Body and Physical Energy

The human body is amazingly adaptive. Its complex structure is made up of many specialized tissues and organs, each of which is made of individual cells. Each cell, however, operates from a common base: No matter the cell's function, it can't perform what it does without energy.[1] If you want to move, energy is required to contract your muscle cells, pull your bony levers, bend your joints. Further, if you want to digest food, the cells of your gastrointestinal system need energy. If you need to concentrate on a difficult task, your brain cells need energy.

Generally, the more physical energy we possess, the better we function. If the energy level is low, cell function is compromised. Think about how your muscles feel after a workout; think about your ability to stay focused if you have not eaten for a prolonged period. We must find a way to bring in more energy before the cells can function fully again.

Almost every cell derives the energy it requires from the union of glucose and oxygen. We get glucose from food we consume, oxygen from the air we breathe. Thus, glucose and oxygen are critical to the functioning and performance of all human beings. Do you find yourself more irritable and impatient when you have not eaten for a long time? It's probably due to low glucose levels. Is it difficult for you to concentrate and focus, for example, when you are hiking or skiing at high altitude or even vacationing high up in the mountains? It's quite likely due to lack of oxygen.

Surely the answer, then, is to eat a large meal and breathe deeply, thus providing your cells with an abundance of glucose and oxygen, which will result in you enjoying a huge influx of physical energy—correct?

Wrong. Think about your last Thanksgiving. You consumed a lot of food, no doubt you breathed a lot—and afterwards you fell into a "food coma" (or at least you became tired and sleepy).

Eating and breathing are not enough. The glucose and oxygen you take in must be transported to cells; not until they reach the cells is there energy production. How does this transport happen? Via blood. The circulation of blood plays a vital role in energy production. Anything which compromises blood flow also compromises energy, in essence your ability to function. If blood flow to part of the heart is blocked, those heart cells are deprived of oxygen (and energy) and a heart attack ensues. If blood flow in or to the brain is blocked, a stroke results. Now, can you think of anything in your life which may impair blood circulation on a daily basis?

How about sitting?

Sitting is an amazingly effective way to impair blood circulation. Your largest muscle, the gluteus maximus (buttocks), contains many blood vessels transporting precious glucose and oxygen to the muscle cells and the rest of the body via the circulatory system. By sitting, you essentially are compressing many of these vessels, thus restricting blood flow. Blood vessels in the thighs, lower back and arms are also compressed. In fact, blood vessels are being compressed in any body part that's pressed against the chair.

Here is what happens next: When you restrict blood flow to a muscle, often the muscle begins to ache. What do you do if you have been sitting for a long period and it becomes physically painful? If you are like most people, you do something often unconsciously. You cross your legs. Why? Because by lifting part of your buttocks off the chair, you allow blood to flow more freely. Soon, discomfort in that part of the buttocks disappears and you are once again sitting more comfortably. After some time, though, you probably find that you are doing something else for no conscious reason: You start to move your suspended foot up and down. Why? Again, to promote blood circulation. Remember, the crossed leg is now pressing on top of your other leg, compressing blood vessels and restricting blood flow to the suspended foot. Eventually, the part of your buttocks that's still on the chair becomes uncomfortable since your weight has been shifted on it. So you switch legs. No wonder so few people can sit still for a prolonged period. It's just too tiring and uncomfortable.

Non-movement such as sitting or standing for prolonged periods eventually becomes a powerful *disengager*. As I discussed, blood circulation is impaired, depriving cells of the precious glucose and oxygen they need to function optimally. But there is more happening. The body is lowering its metabolism to conserve energy (since without movement the demand for energy is low), thus exacerbating feelings of low energy—physically but also emotionally, mentally and possibly spiritually. Muscle tension increases, causing discomfort and still further impairment of blood flow. From then on it is a downward spiral of greater and greater fatigue, discomfort and disengagement.

Let's look at the effects of a long plane ride, like that 8-hour overnight odyssey to England that my girlfriend and I endured. How do you feel after a long flight? Tired? Exhausted? I don't know a person who, after a long flight, would say they feel energized. Most people become drained. But you may wonder, *"Why?"* After all, haven't you just been sitting there, not exerting yourself, maybe cat-napping, occasionally consuming food and drink? Yes—and that's exactly the point. The inactivity, the lack of blood flow, these all eventually deplete your energy. The same principle holds, to an extent, for a long business meeting. Unless you take measures to offset what naturally happens to your circulation and metabolism, your physical energy level will likely decrease as the meeting proceeds. By the end of the meeting you will be emotionally brittle and less mentally alert than you were when you walked into the room. All four dimensions of energy will become more depleted. To stop your slide in productivity, you have to do something. The ideal step would be to stimulate your body in the most powerful way you can.

Move it!

Movement

When you arrive at your destination after a long plane ride, you can sense how much every passenger needs to unbuckle their seatbelt and stand, even before the plane gets safely to the gate. Everyone wants to move, *must* move. It feels great to stretch, better yet to walk—especially if you were sitting in coach, maybe in a middle seat, and your movement was reduced to the occasional squirm.

Human beings were designed to move!

Movement is a powerful way to instantly increase your energy level.[2] As soon as you move, a cascade of physiological and chemical events occurs, which triggers an energy boost.[2,3] The heart rate increases, blood pressure rises, blood vessels dilate to improve blood flow and deliver glucose and oxygen more effectively[1,3]—you instantly increase your metabolism. Movement causes muscles to contract and relax, reducing muscular tension, further enhancing blood flow and alleviating feelings of discomfort. There is more—like the release of hormones such as adrenaline and noradrenalin, which have a powerful, prolonged stimulatory effect on metabolism.[2,3] Move and you very quickly feel more awake, alert, energized, focused, free of discomfort, often happier. And these beneficial effects continue for some time after the movement has stopped.[2,3,4] A 10-minute walk after lunch, for example, improves not only the digestion of the meal but also heightens alertness and focus for 30 minutes or more afterward. A 30-minute workout can boost your energy level for hours afterwards. A good workout in the late afternoon—though you may have started it with low energy—can invigorate you for the rest of the evening; when the effect finally wears off, your body is primed for a terrific night's sleep.

How do *you* typically feel *after* a workout? (Even if you initially didn't want to bother.)

The above examples are about "spot" energizing—moving so that you raise your energy at moments when you seriously need it. (When you are nodding off while driving, it's not the caffeinated coffee or soda you stop to purchase that really helps you to stay awake; the real pick-me-up is getting out of the car, stretching, getting the blood flowing, breathing in the fresh air, walking and then returning to the car.) But if you move not just when you feel you need it (this is often too little, too late!) but rather preemptively throughout the day—often and regularly—you are managing your physical energy and maximizing your performance and productivity. It needn't even be extended or rigorous movement; just movement, plain and simple, provides a surprisingly good bang for the buck, particularly when it's breaking up extended periods of inactivity such as the dreaded mid-afternoon meeting. For instance, standing up—nothing more, just standing up from a sitting position—doubles your metabolic rate![1] Go for even a short walk and you have more than doubled the burn rate again.[1] To prevent mental and emotional disengagement when the muscular system is turned off for prolonged periods—in other words, when you are not moving—even small movements of the hands, feet and arms should be made every 30 to 45 minutes, and large movements such as walking, climbing stairs or full body stretching should be practiced every 90 to 120 minutes. The bigger the range of motion, the better; flexing hand muscles won't stimulate you as much as flexing arm muscles, and so on. Since movement facilitates oxygen transport to the cells and stimulates metabolism, the bigger the movement, the greater the impact. Every time you move a limb, you improve blood circulation to that limb *and* to the brain, which controls that movement,[2] thus increasing alertness, focus and engagement. When sitting for long periods, don't remain statue-like; instead, occasionally take a few deep breaths, flex and extend your ankles, roll your shoulders and change positions on your chair. (Most movements can be done discretely in any situation.) As with food intake, where it's recommended to eat light and often, so, too, it's beneficial to move little and often.

Exercise

As we have seen, all movements, even apparently minor ones, are beneficial to the body and to managing your energy. However, to increase your energy account, you have to increase your fitness. Simply put, increased fitness equals more energy and faster recovery (of energy). It typically means you sleep better, too! There is only one way to increase fitness—exercise! How, then, do we define exercise? Where does small movement end and real exercise begin? Exercise may be defined simply as *any movement that is challenging to the body*—that is, making a movement that falls outside one's "comfort zone."[1] *When exercising, you should not feel comfortable.*

Exercise means exerting yourself. Fortunately, we all have an innate sense of when we are pushing ourselves or not. Alternatively, when working out you should not experience pain; if you do, then you are exerting yourself too much. One rule of thumb: If you can't hold a conversation during aerobic exercise (i.e., running, cycling, swimming), or can't perform at least 8 repetitions of a given weight-lifting exercise, then you are past the discomfort zone and into the pain zone. If that's the case, then pull back. Discomfort, not pain, is what you want to feel.

Comfort: bad. Pain: bad. Discomfort: perfect.

Once you have come up with your preferred exercise(s), then

there are really only three requirements:

- ❑ Exercise outside your comfort zone.
- ❑ Exercise on a regular basis.
- ❑ Be fully engaged when exercising.

At HPI, how do we define "regular basis"? For aerobic exercise, our experience shows that to make a real difference, you must do it at least three times a week[5,6] (if you can do more, great, but it's not required), 30 minutes a session (ditto), with no more than two days of rest in between workouts. For resistance training, we recommend twice a week, on non-consecutive days, one to two sets per exercise, 8 to 12 repetitions,[5,6] with no more than three days of rest in between. Finally, for flexibility training (which people often skip), we recommend three to five days per week, after each exercise session, for at least 5 to 10 minutes, 2 to 5 repetitions per stretch.[5] Stretching is essential as it expands range of motion and offsets the muscle "shortening" that occurs from resistance training. (More extensive exercise guidelines and explanations may be found on the HPI website: www.corporateathlete.com.)

The time commitment is hardly excessive. For a mere 30 minutes a day—and with one or even two days off with no formal exercise—*we guarantee you will see and feel significant improvement in your cardiovascular fitness, strength and flexibility.* Do anything less than the recommended regimen and we can't make that guarantee.

The reason we can guarantee an impact with such little time commitment goes to the third point: *Be engaged when exercising.* Remember, it's not about the time you give to something but the energy—the passion, the commitment, the effort, the engagement. When you exercise, you don't need to give it 2 hours, ever; but you *must* give your focus for the time that you are exercising. The key is to think *quality*, not *quantity*. There is a staggering amount of waste created every day in fitness clubs across America, as seemingly dedicated patrons run on treadmills or climb stair steppers while watching television, reading magazines or talking on their cell phone, not at all connecting with the physical activity they are supposedly "engaged" in. (However, listening to music can enhance exercise intensity.) While I don't discount the other benefits of such an activity—clearing the mind and socializing, to name two—if these lunchtime warriors really wish to condition themselves, they can do so, in far less time, as long as it's concentrated, *intense* time.

We guarantee results provided that you do *not* multitask during your workout, not even in your head. Working out with intensity, with engagement, is the only way to exercise correctly. "I ran three days a week for eight years and my fitness was never all that great," said one client, "but I just kept doing it because it was better than nothing." After coming through our program, he realized that, as long as he was engaged when exercising, he could verify more measurable results *in less time*. "I can really sense how the interval approach helps my heart and stamina and muscle tone so much more," he said. His story is repeated over and over.

Come to your workout to work out, to improve yourself physically—not to (literally) go through the motions. As Dr. Jim Loehr has said: "If a world-class tennis player awaits his opponent's 140 miles-per-hour serve with two thoughts in his head, one of which does not concern how to return a 140-mph serve, his chance of returning that serve successfully is zero percent."

In the meantime, when you are not working out, take the stairs, not the elevator. Take a walk after lunch. Walk to another department rather than e-mailing. Take a shower, not a bath. Avoid drive-through facilities. These are small but meaningful changes you can make during the workday, or just before and after it, to help you boost your energy and reach the next level of conditioning, on your way to a more fit, stronger body. Of course, the benefits of exercise go beyond just enjoying more muscle tone or not having to stop at the third-floor landing to catch your breath on your way to the fifth. A recent study published in *Fitness Matters* showed that employees who worked out not only performed better than those who did not, they also received significantly higher marks for their "intercollea-gual behavior"—respect for their co-workers, a sense of perspective and generally helping to create a better working atmosphere. More proof, once again, that a good foundation of physical energy translates to better emotional, mental and spiritual energy.

Recovery: Maximizing Rest and Sleep

The toughest challenge we have with our predominantly Type A clientele is not getting them to eat correctly or exercise on a regular basis (or at all); it's getting them to strategically disengage. You can't expect to perform at peak if you are always on and never really turned off. (What would happen to a machine that never got turned off?)

As I said, though, our clients are not used to long stretches of inactivity. To them, "downtime" is a four-letter word. From a questionnaire we conduct with all our clients prior to the workshop, we know that more than half of them are "unsuccessful" when it comes to recovery; almost half consider themselves "seriously unsuccessful" when it comes to sleep. Even those who say they are regular about the time they go to bed and wake up admit that the sleep itself is usually not high quality.

Yet all of us, to perform at peak, must honor sleep for what it is: the mechanism by which we fully recover each day. That means going to bed the same time each and every night for 7 to 8 hours of deep sleep.[7] It may mean taking a 30-minute nap each mid-afternoon.[9] We realize that almost no one who comes through our program initially comprehends that. But it's vital to get—in fact, to schedule—sufficient sleep and rest. Without it, not even the most nutritional diet and the most obediently followed exercise regimen can ever fill your tank with the energy you need to achieve maximum performance.

Breaks—either short naps or periods of strategic disengagement during the busy workday—are also vitally important. We recommend that they be taken far more often, roughly one every 90 minutes, than what is typically practiced by most people. After all, world-caliber athletes, the success of whose performance can be judged more precisely and unambiguously perhaps than in any other field of endeavor, build numerous, regular, "intense" breaks into their training because they know that, without them, maximum effort and high-quality execution are impossible.

Cycles of full engagement can best be sustained with brief intervals of recovery (5 to 15 minutes) approximately every 90 minutes. The more fit one is physically, emotionally, mentally and spiritually, the shorter the interval of recovery needed. Speed of recovery is usually an accurate measure of fitness.

What if—as so many of our clients insist is the case—your company frowns on taking breaks? Weak excuse. There are still ways to fit energizing breaks into your workday. One client resolved this by setting his watch to ring an alert on the hour, at which point he stands, drinks water and keeps working for 5 minutes *while standing*; another client decided always to take a short walk down the hall after finishing one type of work and before starting another; another client built in at least three 5-minute breaks during the day—at 10:30 a.m., 1:30 p.m. and 4:30 p.m.—to meet a colleague in front of the office and bask briefly in sunlight.

Because we generally don't give the concept of recovery its proper due, when people actually do it, they do it poorly. For example, how often has this happened? After a ridiculously busy day at work you are totally exhausted, you lie down in bed...and you can't sleep.

Odd. Why would that be? Just when you need recovery *most*, the mechanism controlling it suddenly doesn't work? One explanation is that, as anyone who regularly exercises knows, the more physically fit you are, the deeper and better you tend to sleep[8] (called delta sleep); thus, the quality of one's recovery (disengagement) is directly linked to the quality of one's physical exercise (engagement). In short, the beneficial effects of exercise continue even after you stop, even while you are asleep! On the other hand, for those who are not so fit and, more crucially, who rarely engage fully in what they are doing, it's simply harder to switch completely off, because they are never switched completely on.

Please resist the urge to think you are so special that you simply don't need the time (or can't take the time) to rejuvenate, and that you will somehow still manage to get things accomplished, and completed well, on insufficient rest. If you have told yourself this (maybe for years), then you are simply kidding yourself. To maintain optimal efficiency, the average man or woman must be in sleep mode approximately one-third of every 24 hours. (Highly fit individuals may require fewer than 8 hours.)[8] And, as stated before, going to bed early and waking up early, as well as going to bed and getting up consistently at the same time, will give you more energy than going to bed and waking up late, or sleeping at inconsistently set intervals.

Move and exercise regularly to manage and increase energy, respectively. Take small breaks throughout the day and sleep adequately at night to recover energy. Without this cycle of stress/recovery, it's simply impossible to perform at your best. With it, along with proper nutrition, you will experience unprecedented levels of energy, productivity and fulfillment. We guarantee it.

PART II: APPLICATIONS

Chapter 4

The Research Case for the Corporate Athlete

by Dr. Jack Groppel

In 1981, I was sitting in a seminar about improving performance led by Stan Smith, who at the time was nearing the end of a brilliant tennis career, during which he had won Wimbledon and U.S. Open singles titles, had been ranked number one in the world, and had proved himself one of the greatest doubles players in history. I was there because I was interested in what a great champion like Stan had to say about world-class performance.

With the main portion of the evening over, there was time for Q&A and one of the audience members raised his hand. "Mr. Smith, now that you are in the twilight of your playing career," he asked, "what do you plan to do next?"

Without missing a beat, Stan said, "I plan on taking what I learned as a competitor and using it in my business."

To you, what Stan said may seem an utterly obvious direction. For me, at that moment, it felt like an epiphany. *Of course,* I thought. Why wouldn't you fully exploit the lessons, techniques and approach that helped make you a phenomenally successful performer in the world of sport? *There is a great performer in all of us albeit in sport or business*, I thought; and, in the business world we might best think of ourselves as "Corporate Athletes."

At that time, Jim Loehr and I had been friends for several years, and we had been searching for ways to bring together our respective strengths for a new business. Like myself, Jim had been a serious collegiate tennis player and had spent the past several years working with athletes. When I wasn't teaching and conducting research at the University of Illinois, I was at the U.S. Olympic Training Center in Colorado Springs, where I used my background in biomechanics, kinesiology, nutrition and exercise physiology to research elite performances of our top athletes. Jim, meanwhile, with his background in psychology, was not just coaching top tennis players and athletes in other sports but pioneering the landmark idea that human beings are, at the most basic level, complex energy systems. In essence, Jim's entire career has been dedicated to the understanding of energy management. Both of us believed that there was value, perhaps great value, in applying sport science principles to human performance in *all* aspects of life. As much as we enjoyed working with athletes, we grew confident that our formulations could have a profound, even transformative, effect on high-level performers from virtually any arena of life and, in turn, on their organizations. In fact, it was in the vast, highly competitive world of business where we thought the application of our training model could potentially have its greatest impact.

There is a great performer in all of us. Jim and I knew as well as anyone that the best athletes in the world succeeded because they knew how to manage their energy better than their competitors. By doing that, they coped with and even thrived in high-stress situations. It seemed only logical that it would work in other high-stress arenas as well. Soon after, we attracted the FBI as a client. Then came elite anti-terrorist units and Navy SEALS, and men and women from local law enforcement. The principles of energy management seemed to have been designed for them; it was almost hard to imagine that these concepts were first and foremost cultivated for athletes.

More and more of our clients, though, were coming from the world of business, and across every segment: telecommunications, financial services, retail, pharmaceuticals, manufacturing, hospitality, transportation, consulting and insurance. If we didn't fully acknowledge the level of stress that typical business people faced every day—and we did—and if we didn't fully appreciate how connected organizational profitability and total success were to its workforce's energy level—and we did—then we certainly understood it now. As we came to hear more of their stories, hear more of their frustrations and appreciated more of their desires to have greater work/life balance, to perform at peak for the greatest amount of time, and to be in control of their professional—and personal—destinies, the connection became alarmingly clear.

Today, 80 percent of our clientele comes from the traditional business arena. We can now say, 30 years after we met, that we were absolutely right in this key supposition: The principles of energy management can bring great value to business people everywhere. It was this original supposition that explains why we made energy management the key component to becoming a great corporate athlete. It's also why we have succeeded in watching our clients return to their jobs and their lives with a new understanding of what they must do to take their game, professional and personal, to the next level. And why we have seen so many clients return to their lives and stop smoking, lose weight, eat better, exercise more, interact more—and deeply—with their families, reinvigorate friendships, pursue dreams, stop procrastinating...and perform at work better than they have ever performed before.

Once, at a leadership meeting for a Fortune 100 company, I listened as an executive said to his team, "You have 24 hours in the day and there are three things you must be concerned with: your job, your family and yourself. I can do only two. For me, it has always been my job and my family. I have always put myself on the backburner."(As you will learn throughout this book, this is not a sustainable mindset!)

At a different company, another executive asked me, "Why is guilt so rampant in the business world? And how do you coach people to deal with it?" I asked him what he felt guilty about. "Being away from home and exercising," he said. He even felt guilty if his lunchtime was anything more than eating on the run; that extra time, he felt, could be going to bettering his productivity. So he felt guilty when he wasn't working, and he felt guilty when the work hours got long, as they frequently did, because that meant he was spending too little time at home with his family.

Obviously, there are some incompatible forces here. So many executives and other employees operate in *unsustainable* situations—unsustainable, that is, if they hope to live long, healthy, fulfilled lives. So how does the individual resolve this? As you are likely aware, this has been addressed throughout the first part of this book: Jim Loehr introduced the energy management model that he pioneered, where he talked about the individual's need to manage energy wisely so that he or she can be fully engaged; and about how the quality, quantity, focus and force of our energy supply affects us not just physically but also emotionally, mentally and spiritually. Raquel Malo and Chris Jordan, likewise, imparted information on how to deepen engagement through nutrition and movement.

In the rest of this chapter I am concerned less with the individual and more with the employer, and the state of organizational culture. In doing so, I believe it will become evident that most of the business world—and I'm sure your own work experience can attest to this—is suffering. I believe it will also become apparent that a new mindset is needed—namely, the corporate athlete solution, whose principles and successful application are highly relevant, across a wide range of industries.

What Research Data Depicts

While study after study shows that healthier and more fulfilled employees translate to a robust bottom line, the business world has struggled to find real-life, practical ways to support this understanding. The workplace is far too often stressful and dispiriting, but precious little, in few businesses, is being done to improve the situation. According to the Centers for Disease Control, more than 75 percent of employer healthcare costs and productivity losses are related to employee lifestyle choices[1]—however, according to a 2006 study published in the *American Journal of Health Promotion,* less than 20 percent of U.S. employers offer lifestyle modification services.[2]

Stress—much of it work-related—has been implicated in 60 to 90 percent of medical problems, yet the fallout goes way beyond just healthcare costs. Here are some of the many ways in which stressed out employees impact their organization's health—and, collectively, the culture itself:

1. *Absenteeism.* In a study in the *American Journal of Health Promotion*, workers experiencing high stress were more than twice as likely to be absent more than five times per year.[3]
2. *Workers compensation claims.* Nine of ten stress claimants receive compensation benefits; job pressures account for nearly seven of ten stress claims. And stress-related claims have jumped several multiples in the past generation.[3]
3. *Litigation.* According to *The American Workers Under Pressure Technical Report*, "Discovering specific stressors and dealing with them is by far the best course of action for organizations. There is a better likelihood of litigation if a company ignores stress-related problems than if it addresses them up front."[3]
4. *Grievances.* In one study, each filed grievance translated into roughly 80 hours of lost productivity—accounting not only for the worker filing the grievance but also the morale of those around him.[3]
5. *Turnover.* According to the Bureau of National Affairs, 40 percent of employee turnover is related to stress.[3]
6. *Accidents.* Workers who report high stress are 30 percent more likely to have accidents than those with low stress. *The Harvard Business Review* reports that stress-related accident claims are, on average, two times more costly than non-stress-related cases.[3]
7. *Errors in judgment and action.* Stressed out workers become preoccupied with the issues troubling them; such tunnel vision dulls thinking, increasing the chance for making often costly mistakes.[3]
8. *Conflict and interpersonal problems.* When under extreme stress, employees are less likely to respond constructively, heightening the chance they will find their surroundings even more difficult and depleting.[3]
9. *Customer service problems.* The connection between happy employees and satisfied customers is obvious but often ignored—and stressed out employees virtu-

ally guarantee alienation of customers. According to a study of over 100 companies in *The Harvard Business Review,* a mere 5 percent reduction in customer defection translates into a 30 to 85 percent increase in profitability.[4] Thus, even a relatively small percentage of customers who are not completely satisfied with a company's service can result in a huge loss in profitability.

10. *Resistance to change.* Many companies fail in their attempt at organizational change because the employees resist the change. As a person's stress level increases, he or she is more likely to respond in a more primitive, hard-wired way—that is, to cling, where possible, to old ways and go into survival mode. Research shows that stress is connected to neophobia, a fear of novelty.[3]

11. *Loss of intellectual capital.* Organizations thrive when they are perceptive, nimble and responsive to market demands and customer need. Unfortunately, a workforce under high stress—in other words, the majority of organizations—make these virtues close to impossible. The more stressed out the workers, the less they care about excellence and innovation. The driving force is survival.[3]

If it wasn't apparent before that stress is a widespread, undeniable force in the life of employees, it should be now. Since stress is so often such a powerful destabilizing force in the workplace, I would like to reiterate how stress is conceptualized within our corporate athlete model. As Jim Loehr noted in *Chapter 1,* according to our model, the real culprit in terms of risks to the health and well-being of employees is not, in fact, stress exposure but rather *chronic* stress exposure. The real problem is the insufficiency of periodic recovery to balance the stress. World-class stress creates the opportunity for world-class growth as long as adequate recovery is provided. In practical terms, work/life balance is actually stress/recovery balance. All stress becomes dysfunctional without periodic recovery. Within our corporate athlete model, stress is simply defined as energy expenditure. Stress can occur on physical, emotional, mental and spiritual levels because energy can be expended in each of these areas. Balance occurs when energy out (stress) is equivalent to energy in (recovery). The rhythm of energy out and energy in creates the pulse of life. Energy expenditure is the stimulus for all growth and energy renewal is when growth actually takes place. Excessive stress relative to recovery or excessive recovery relative to stress leads to distress and dysfunctionality. Learning how to balance cycles of stress with cycles of recovery—physically, emotionally, mentally and spiritually is at the very heart of the energy management technology. Most of the disengagement problems connected to workplace stress are attributable to stress/recovery imbalances.

The following statistics revealed in a survey conducted by Oxford Health Plans point to workplace practices that undermine recovery:[5]

❑ One in six U.S. employees is so overworked that they are unable to use up annual vacation time, despite the fact that Americans have the least vacation time in the industrialized world.

❑ One in three American workers reports they have such pressing jobs that they have no downtime at work.

❑ One in three never leaves the building once they arrive at work.

❑ One in seven believes management only promotes people who habitually work late.

❑ One in five says workplace pressures make them believe they must attend work even when sick or injured.

❑ One in six says it is difficult to take time off or leave work in an emergency.

❑ One in roughly twelve believes that if they were to become seriously ill, they would be fired or demoted.

To summarize, a 2003 survey by Management Recruiters International noted that, out of 730 executives, 35 percent had too much work to take a vacation and that 47 percent expected to make fewer vacation plans.[6] They decided to stay at work and use their vacation time to get caught up on their increased workloads. So, yes, chronic stress deeply affects the individual suffering. As already stated, stress unabated by recovery compromises a person's physical, mental and emotional capacity, and erodes his or her very motivation.

It is all rather strange to demand such great quantities of high-quality energy and effort from workers yet provide so little opportunity to recover the expended energy. After all, a major portion of a corporation's assets is its intellectual capital—the knowledge, skills and abilities of the employees. A company loses money each time one of these employees ceases to be motivated—and they do so far more often when they get closer to burnout. Burnout, essentially, is energy bankruptcy. One study shows that turnover can cost as much as four times the departing person's salary.[7] And with the workforce aging, the energy problem will only get more challenging, not less.

The results of an eight-year study found a "relationship between physical inactivity and cognitive decline" across all subgroups.[8] The sedentary lives of corporate workers result in insufficient physical stress and that energy imbalance negatively impacts cognitive performance. The results also discovered "a 'dose' relationship between exercise and mental alertness—a little exercise is good, but more is better," as long as adequate recovery is provided.

These Times Call for Extraordinary Solutions

I refer you to a quote from the Director of Benefits of the Total Compensation Group at Scotiabank, "Many companies face the challenge of articulating what wellness means to an organization. Most define wellness in the form of activities and events."[9] Since wellness has conventionally been viewed as a "soft" form of dollars spent, we present the corporate athlete solution as the long-term plan that can provide employers with measurable, bottom-line outcomes. In the chapters that follow, the individual and organizational benefits of this technology will be delineated in considerable detail. As will be made clear throughout the second part of this publication, our corporate athlete training system improves shareholder value from two perspectives: higher performance from a more loyal workforce, and lower cost because of improved preventive care.

By embedding our energy management technology into the corporate culture, forward-thinking organizations find that employees are more satisfied, more productive and perhaps less likely to defect. The benefits of employee satisfaction, commitment and retention far outweigh the expenses of incorporating the energy management technology.

It has been written that investment in human capital grows over time just as monetary investments. But the behaviors of many organizations aren't congruent with this. In a 2007 survey by Monster, Canadian employees were asked, "Does your company offer corporate wellness programs such as fitness/nutritional coaching, fitness club memberships, training seminars, etc.?" Out of 2,857 responses, 68 percent said "No, but I wish they did."[9]

The Good News

If I'm going to throw alarming statistics at you, then it's only fair that I share some inspiring ones at you as well. The business case for wellness programs is overwhelmingly positive:

- ❏ One study found that employers could, through comprehensive health and productivity programs, reduce their cost per employee by 26 percent.[10]
- ❏ One Forbes 100 company (DuPont) found that each dollar invested in workplace health promotion yielded US$1.42 over two years (in lower absenteeism costs).[11]
- ❏ Another major firm claimed a US$3.40 return for every dollar invested in health promotion, yielding total corporate savings of US$146 million in benefits costs. In addition, over four years, sick leave was reduced by 19 percent.[12]
- ❏ A top insurance company lowered its medical costs by almost half for each participant in its wellness program.[13]
- ❏ Another company instituted a "Stay Alive and Well Program," in which over half of its 1,600 employees participated. Over two years, those who did experienced significantly lower cholesterol levels and blood pressure; and lifestyle-related claim costs dropped significantly for the participants compared to non-participants.[14]

❑ A major bank saved almost US$6 for every dollar spent on worksite wellness.[15] This type of return on investment (ROI) has been seen across the industry. In 2008, U.S. Corporate Wellness, Inc. published an Executive Summary which stated: "A growing number of employers are taking a preventative approach to these costs by providing employee wellness programs as a standard employee benefit. The research clearly demonstrates that by encouraging healthier choices among their current employees, they are reaping long-term savings in terms of sick time, disability and healthcare costs. Further ROI analysis demonstrates that these measurables are only a portion of the cost savings. In reality, companies that have effectively developed a wellness culture also realize cost savings in reference to retention, recruitment, reputation and employee 'presenteeism' (engagement)."[16]

❑ Mental performance has been found to be significantly better in physically fit workers than in non-fit workers. In one study, fit workers committed 27 percent fewer errors on tasks involving concentration and short-term memory, as compared with the performance of non-fit workers.[17]

❑ It was reported in the *Journal of Applied Psychology* that workers who have more control over their hours are less likely to experience work/life balance frustrations. They continued to say that high-control jobs are generally better for one's health than jobs where employees perceive little control.[18]

❑ WebMD reported in 2005 that social pressures that exist in many corporate environments actually promote weight gain.[19] Not only is it part of corporate culture to eat high-caloric and unhealthy foods that are readily available, but there are also the ever-present vending machines with poor selections. In fact, constant business stress without relief causes one to skip meals, then to consume meals hurriedly (when one does eat) and to marginalize exercise in the daily regimen.[20]

What does all this mean? That organizations providing opportunities for exercise, healthy meals and snacks, strategic breaks and, in general, high-quality recovery will thrive, or thrive to a greater extent than those that do not. Employee retention is higher for exercisers than non-exercisers. (Interestingly, even those who don't exercise often view the health and fitness center benefit as a symbol of corporate concern and goodwill!) Furthermore, attitude, morale and job satisfaction increase: Those who participate in programs report increased alertness and better rapport with their coworkers.

And, finally, there is the bottom-line effect: Performance and productivity rise, measurably. In one large-scale survey, job performance strongly correlated with exercise adherence: Those who received the highest performance ratings from supervisors were most likely to adhere to exercise programs. A NASA study reported a 12.5 percent increase in productivity for people who exercise regularly.[21] Exercisers worked at full efficiency for the entire day, while non-exercising employees lost 50 percent efficiency for the final 2 hours. Participants demonstrated increased stamina, performance, concentration and decision-making abilities. In a nine-month analysis of decision-making capabilities, exercisers showed a distinct advantage (70 percent greater performance) over non-exercisers.[22] Another study found that employees who took part in their organization's health promotion plans displayed significant improvement in the categories of organizational commitment, supervision, working conditions, job competence, job security and benefits.[23]

Dr. Kenneth Pelletier, a pioneer in the field of worksite health promotion, has reviewed dozens of corporate wellness research papers over the last two decades. His conclusions have been that "the vast majority of the research to date indicates positive clinical and cost outcomes."[24]

It seems clear that a sizeable portion of the billions of dollars currently spent by employers on health-related costs would cease if businesses would offer its workforce more extensive health promotion programming and better nutrition, and focused more attention on employee work/life balance and other stress factors. These programs are cost-effective and cut across a spectrum of needs. To keep workers fulfilled, respected and relevant, quite a few organizations provide ongoing training and education.[16,23,24,25] More traditionally and modestly, some organizations offer fitness club memberships and field employee sports teams.

So the obvious question is how does the corporate athlete solution connect to all this? The answer is simple and direct. It provides both a framework for understanding the vast array of health and wellness issues impacting worker productivity as well as offers a highly unique and effective technology for initiating individual and organizational change. The solution this technology ultimately delivers is *helping employees manage their energy more skillfully.* Issues of burnout, excessive stress, concentration problems, presenteeism, disengagement, low morale and poor health are, at the most basic level, traceable to deficiencies in energy management. Some of the most prestigious business schools in the world are already beginning to embrace the link between energy management and business performance. Consequently, I was appointed as an Adjunct Professor of Management to teach our technology within the Executive Master's Programs at Northwestern's Kellogg School of Management. Additionally, Jim Loehr has taught HPI's corporate athlete solution to the entire MBA Program at the University of Michigan.

Enhancing Engagement
Whenever leaders offer real solutions for helping their workers better balance the demands of their professional and personal lives, employees' willingness to invest effort and energy increase (their engagement deepens). These organizations tend to enjoy fewer absences and disability claims, lower health insurance costs and higher productivity. How much, you ask? Taking all the numbers from the various studies and organizations, it appears that investment in a modest health promotion program costs a mid-sized company somewhere in the neighborhood of US$500 per employee per year, and yields about a 3:1 return.[26]

For a program to be truly effective, of course, there needs to be widespread participation. But given that employees are increasingly demanding a balance between work and family life, and are not willing to sacrifice everything for their careers and employers, firms would be wise to meet them part way. For a plan to have *sustainability* within an organization, there needs to be a plan in place that is user-friendly and has accountability. After 30 years of studying human behavior and the process around change, the Human Performance Institute is dedicated to teaching people not only how to manage their energy but to sustain it throughout their entire life. The only way to create long-term positive outcomes is to inaugurate a program that can support employees in the most comprehensive manner.

What's your gut reaction to the following scenario?

- ❑ 10 minutes of free massage therapy each week.
- ❑ Tuition reimbursement for one class.
- ❑ Some flex time.
- ❑ Casual dress opportunities.
- ❑ Three days of community leave per year.

However superfluous as these perks may sound to you, they go a long way toward producing healthier, happier, better energy-balanced employees.

Just to demonstrate that this is not wishful thinking: A company that offered each and every one of the perks above (except it was *15* minutes of massage therapy, it was tuition reimbursement for *any* class, and it was *12* days of community leave per year) reduced its turnover rate from 20 percent, the industry average, to 5 percent![27]

Specific Research Utilizing HPI's Corporate Athlete Model

Since 2003, GlaxoSmithKline has offered our energy management curriculum to their employees. They have utilized our train-the-trainer program and have been delivering the content internally with their own facilitators. In GSK's own evaluation of the program over the last several years[28], they acknowledged, "This program is a highly practical, scientifically-based approach to increasing performance by more skillfully managing energy. Above all, the program provides the tools to aid participants in building the skills and capacity to remain fully engaged and perform at their best regardless of the conditions."

The following summarizes GSK's own internal research on HPI's energy management curriculum and its effects on their employees:

- ❑ Significant positive behavioral changes were observed and these changes were shown to be *sustainable* from the time of initial training and when measured over a year after the training occurred.

- ❏ 97 percent of the respondents to GSK's follow-up metrics would recommend the training program to others.
- ❏ In response to questions regarding "level of improvement," the following data was obtained:
  - 82 percent said they had increased their physical energy levels.
  - 89 percent said they had increased their emotional resilience.
  - 87 percent said they had increased their mental capacity.
  - 80 percent said they had increased their spiritual capacity (defined as the ability to align yourself with your deepest values).

Additional data is equally promising. In a follow-up assessment of HPI's two-and-a-half-day executive course, independently conducted by Performance Programs, Inc., the observations for all clients coming through included:[29]

- ❏ When asked how successful the participants had been in their overall engagement *since their training course*, 96.5 percent responded that they had experienced success.
- ❏ 93.5 percent said they had been successful at improving their physical energy.
- ❏ 94.1 percent said they had been successful at improving their emotional energy.
- ❏ 97.5 percent said they had been successful at improving their mental energy.
- ❏ 92.5 percent said they had been successful at improving their spiritual energy.
- ❏ 97.5 percent said they had seen improvement in engagement with their own health.
- ❏ 83.3 percent said they often, almost always or always have high physical energy at work.
- ❏ 89.6 percent said they often, almost always or always are mentally alert at work.
- ❏ 91.5 percent said they often, almost always or always

feel effective in their work role.

❑   90.5 percent said they often, almost always or always persevere in the face of obstacles.

❑   84.7 percent said they often, almost always or always are resilient under emotional pressure.

❑   84.6 percent said they often, almost always or always felt fully engaged at work.

This data suggests very positive results from participation in HPI executive courses; not just at work, but effects can extend to increased capacity for engagement in all aspects of life.

In a 2008 study published in the *Journal of Correctional Health Care*, Dr. Mark Anshel and Dr. Minsoo Kang examined the effects of HPI's energy management technology on 67 police officers. They studied the effects of a 10-week energy management intervention on selected measures of fitness, blood lipids (reflecting changes in exercise and dietary habits) and exercise adherence. They found a marked improvement in health behaviors among the participants.[30]

Published in 2007 in *Behavioral Medicine*, Anshel and Kang also utilized HPI's energy management curriculum to examine how having a disconnect from one's values affects efficacy and success in behavioral health improvement. The investigation was conducted with 51 college faculty members, again employing a 10-week intervention. Significant improvements in *all* fitness and lipid profiles were observed. 88 percent of the participants viewed the program as highly favorable and 100 percent agreed that HPI's corporate athlete model (regarding identifying their values and the disconnect that might exist) was self-motivating when making the commitment to an exercise program.[31]

In further examination of the data obtained in the above participant group, Anshel and Kang published the following findings in June 2007 in the *Consulting Psychology Journal*.[32] They employed HPI's *Full Engagement 360 Profile* to examine how the 10-week intervention replaced unhealthy behaviors with health-enhancing rituals that could be sustained. Their analysis revealed statistically significant improvement from the pre-intervention scores to the post-intervention scores on physical, emotional, mental, spiritual and recovery metrics. It was postulated that a likely explanation of such positive outcomes was that, in addition to a change in exercise habit (reported in the *Behavioral Medicine* study from the previous paragraph), participants also incorporated total lifestyle changes based on HPI's energy management curriculum.

In summary, due to the entrenched culture of most high-stress venues, workers may be willing but, without training, simply unable to meet the expanding demands of their lives. These are extraordinary times, for sure, that call for extraordinary measures. For us at the Human Performance Institute, that extraordinary measure is a solution that links worker productivity with worker health and well-being. This is precisely what happens when energy is positioned as the fundamental currency of high performance. Issues of productivity, health and happiness are inexorably linked to the skillful management of energy and we need look no further than the high stakes world of professional sport to deepen our understanding of what skillful energy management really means.

Chapter 5

Could This Be the Solution to Our Healthcare Crisis?

by Dr. Leo Greenstone

The American healthcare system is, as a rule, very good at taking care of those who are acutely ill and supporting those who are chronically ill. It is not particularly good at preventing people from *becoming* ill. Much of this may be explained through education and incentives (or lack of). When I was in medical school, we were taught about diseases—not about prevention, health or wellness. Later, as a physician, I had an incentive to diagnose disease, since I would be reimbursed for my services. Few insurance companies genuinely support health maintenance; if they did, then they would be reimbursing healthcare providers who educate the population on how to stay healthy (a starkly different proposition from educating the population on what to do once you become sick). Some insurance companies pay for more preventive services, early screening tests and procedures, but very few pay for broader nutrition and fitness services. Individuals are not strongly encouraged to use exercise physiologists and nutritionists, whose programs promote health and wellness (even if they were encouraged, there is no clear infrastructure that supports such activities as medically indicated), as they are not really *treating* a medical condition and are not therefore reimbursable. True, many organizations offer their employees wellness programs.

However, without measurement and real accountability—and a medical culture that values working at maintaining good health, not just combating sickness—it's naïve to expect significant numbers will ever avail themselves of these programs.

Consider instead, if we focused much more on *preventing* ill health? Two out of three chronic diseases are *preventable*; three of four premature deaths are *preventable*.[1] Simple math tells us that if we made a significant impact on these numbers, the ripple would be enormous. Think of the improved physical and psychological well-being of millions of people; of the decrease in obesity, diabetes and numerous other conditions, in adults and children; of the benefit derived from the millions of loved ones of these newly or continually healthy people; of the countless organizations that would now thrive, rather than collapse—as so many are on the verge of, weighed down by their increased healthcare-related costs; of the improved financial health of the nation, whose financial burden from healthcare continues to increase, and to cripple?

If such a reasonable, prevention-first solution were that simple and available, we would have implemented it by now, right? After all, the data is clear: People with healthy lifestyle behaviors live longer, healthier, more productive lives. The formula for good health—proper nutrition, exercise and rest—is simple. And yet...it's difficult for most of us to implement. A massive national study (164,940 adults surveyed!) on healthy lifestyles revealed that less than 3 percent of us actually participate in all the healthy behaviors in question.[2] Then again, it's not as if Americans avoid attempts to live healthier. Witness the staggering number of diet and self-help books, a new one appearing seemingly every hour. More than half of all Americans say they have tried to lose weight in the past year.[3]

From the work perspective, few organizations have succeeded in achieving a real impact. So far, the available wellness programs are used by only a small fraction of employees. Despite all the proven benefits, even in some of the top executive wellness programs, with enormously successful and supposedly well-informed clients, less than 30 percent follow the detailed prescription for good health and make the necessary lifestyle changes. Could it be that these programs fail to connect health and wellness with the ability to achieve and sustain peak performance and happiness? Could it be that the typical executive definition of success forbids one from making real change to a system (one's own body, one's own self) that, after all, *somehow* must work correctly—for how could the executive have reached the hilltop in the first place?

In both the corporate world and the individual's world beyond the office, there are gaping deficiencies: on-going support, sufficient incentives, appropriate tools and the proper habits necessary for employees to make positive, healthy changes. I mean, *really* make them. And really stick to them.

Could the corporate athlete solution be the answer to this giant problem? Certainly no one system or idea, no matter how big or effective or paradigm-busting, can solve the American healthcare dilemma in its entirety. Over 40 million Americans are uninsured, with very limited access to healthcare. The United States spends nearly 17 percent of its Gross Domestic Product on healthcare, yet the World Health Organization ranks us only 37th in the world in overall health of our citizens.[4,5] Our problems clearly will not and cannot be solved quickly.

And that's what I especially respect about the corporate athlete solution: It's decidedly *not* a quick-fix design but rather a comprehensive, broadly implemented program that demands meaningful buy-in from the individual, that understands the necessity to engage Corporate America in the effort, and that doesn't contend real change can be achieved or sustained if it's all about a single-minded focus on the physical body.

I went through the corporate athlete solution workshop myself. As a practicing clinician interested in providing the very best care for his patients suffering with numerous diseases, and as a physician interested in preventing my patients from having to suffer in the first place, I found the corporate athlete solution to be a profoundly powerful tool that could assist *all* my patients to accomplish their goals.

The majority of insured Americans receive healthcare coverage through private employer-sponsored group health insurance, and Corporate America contributes a significant portion. A recent study showed that over 90 percent of companies with 100+ workers offer some form of wellness program to their employees.[6] If these companies expanded their wellness programs to include energy management principles—and were able to promote those compelling ideas that make the corporate athlete solution so effective where other, supposedly similar wellness programs fail—I am certain that productivity, profitability and morale would increase exponentially, while absenteeism and presenteeism (on-the-job productivity loss) would plummet.

Earlier in the book, the principles behind the corporate athlete solution were spelled out, so I won't revisit the science. Still many programs have sound science. But sound science alone will not convince you suddenly to re-fashion your habits and re-number your priorities in one evening, so that the next morning you are living healthier. What I contend distinguishes the corporate athlete solution from other programs—and maybe this sounds radical coming from a medical doctor—is the link between the lifestyle changes necessary for good health (on the one hand) to one's sense of self and, further, to one's core values (on the other). This connection is ever-present. The corporate athlete solution insists that you examine the *meaning* and *purpose* of your life. It asks you to reflect deeply on what is important.

At every step of my corporate athlete training course, I saw a direct connection between the teaching and the potential outcome. The instructors made easy and practical what I, as a physician, knew to be quite complicated. To begin, there *was* the sound science: The training focused on how to establish and maintain good eating habits, and how to better understand food portions and food composition and its relationship to energy. Participants learned how to use this new knowledge about nutrition to produce more as well as higher quality energy. Trainers explained the basics of portion control, how to use and manage the glycemic index, how and why to consume certain snacks for maximum energy. They talked about how eating for energy (something all top athletes, of course, understand) is the same as, and different from, eating for health.

Exercise? The corporate athlete solution trainers help participants create personalized, realizable workout regimens. They taught the effect such workouts would likely have on cardiovascular fitness, cholesterol levels, immune system function and more. They taught how resistance training increased metabolism (and of course showed correct and wrong techniques), and how to manage blood sugar levels.

In the end, the largely corporate clientele in my group learned that proper diet, cardiovascular exercise, resistance training and proper recovery all improve one's energy; and that, by accomplishing these the correct way, with the correct amount and at the correct time, they also improve one's health.

But we all more or less knew that, didn't we?

What the corporate athlete solution does to truly compel participants, to truly motivate us, is to link these health measures and the consequent benefits with one's overall values and goals.

I was struck by how moved I and the other participants became when we were challenged to ask ourselves the question, "Are you living in ways that are truly consistent with your core values, with the things you *say* are most important to you?" We were then asked to link our core values with our newly desired habits and behaviors.

Soon enough I could see that this approach would not only help all of us in the room but also my patients—and my medical colleagues. As a profession, physicians suffer among the highest divorce rate, suicide rate and substance abuse rate; far too many of us manage our energy and health poorly, or fail to provide ourselves with the care necessary to perform at our best.[7] Physicians are often overworked and stressed. And while many of us have intuitively figured out habits that enable us to perform well under pressure situations—it happens all the time in emergency and operating rooms—we rarely appreciate the importance of recovery and rejuvenation in sustaining high performance over time. Like it or not, physicians are role models for their patients—and veteran physicians are role models for young physicians in training. If we cannot personally demonstrate, and thus promote, good health and healthy lifestyle practices, how dare we prescribe it? And expect to convince others that it is achievable? We must create environments in which young people *want to work*. As healers, many of us need to embrace the energy management principles in our work lives, in the operating room and in our lives outside the office. One would hope that such a radically new approach by physicians and other medical practitioners would have a large-scale salutary effect throughout the healthcare system.

Physicians are not the only profession, of course, that could benefit significantly from the corporate athlete solution. During my corporate athlete solution workshop, I understood immediately how just about *every* professional ought to go through this type of training—particularly those who perform under pressure, where energy and engagement are essential. I would go so far to say that every professional school in America should provide their students with the corporate athlete solution. After all, when our future leaders enter the professional world, they would benefit profoundly if they understood how and why to remain healthy, and thus productive, for the many years of their careers. As more captains of industry learn about, understand and finally adopt the basic principles that the corporate athlete solution promotes—namely, that real success happens not by managing time but by managing energy, and that extraordinary success happens when we manage extraordinary energy (and they create rigorous programs for all of their employees based on the energy management principles)—we will see a virtual epidemic of good health break out across Corporate America. The robust good health of the bottom line will definitely be realized.

The corporate athlete solution works for the individual. But it also helps the individual organization and, dare I say, will help the nation, too. I don't believe the claim is unrealistical. If this program and its principles are introduced into the healthy corporate environment, which usually insists on accountability, then the impact will be profound, especially where businesses want to encounter it most: return on investment (ROI).

Most large corporations have established some kind of corporate wellness program. Johnson and Johnson, Dow and Pfizer, to name three, have enjoyed positive ROI from their initiatives. One study showed that, for every dollar spent on such programs, some organizations save between five and seven dollars![8] The numbers vary with "high-risk" versus "low-risk" employees, the effectiveness of particular programs and the power of the incentive. (With most organizations, participation is voluntary.) The most successful programs target workers at risk for developing work-related injuries and illnesses that decrease productivity and increase absenteeism. Assessments of blood pressure, body mass index (BMI), cholesterol levels, asking workers about sedentary life style, smoking, self-perception of poor health status and life dissatisfaction identify those at highest risk, and thus, those most likely to benefit the most from such programs.

Fortunately, there is now considerable movement in our culture to increase awareness of prevention, to provide Americans with healthier choices and support programs. Many school systems are, finally, removing vending machines that appeared to have been placed in cafeterias solely to dispense high-fat snacks and high-sugar drinks to American children and teens and, in so doing, helping to increase the percentage of our youth suffering (to name the most insidious results) from obesity and diabetes. Schools are also re-evaluating the need—ignored for many years—for mandatory physical education. Fast food restaurants, amazingly, are offering salads, healthy (or at least *healthier*) sandwiches and wraps. More health and fitness clubs are emerging. More organizations are starting wellness programs, many of which aim to help employees to stop smoking, to start exercising, to eat correctly. Some organizations provide fitness centers at the worksite, while others pay for health club memberships.

But that is also part of the problem: The vast majority of these programs focus on physical aspects only. Corporate leaders are, for the most part, alarmingly uneducated about the need for an integrated approach to health and wellness. I served as Medical Director of an executive health program for two years, and assessed the health and health risks of numerous C-level executives. While I had a tough time convincing many of them about the need for regular physical exercise and good nutrition, it was far more difficult getting them to connect their own values with such activities, and vice versa. Even the most esteemed wellness programs I encountered—before learning of the corporate athlete solution—have failed in this way. Few wellness programs that I have seen acknowledge the emotional and spiritual components of being human. Yet, perhaps somewhat ironically, we know to our core that people really have to care about the "why" before they can seriously begin to change, and to change successfully. What is more, they need tools to implement new behaviors and habits into their lives—tools that are accessible and practical and intuitive but that also strike a deep chord.

Of course, the corporate athlete solution begins by assessing individual *physical*, medical risks: It measures basic indicators, evaluates the information provided on the health questionnaire, and then translates it all into individualized recommendations for action. Where the corporate athlete solution is unique is this: It promotes the idea that, while we all want the best, most energy to manage, energy is not a single type. Rather, it is physical, emotional, mental and spiritual energy. They are not separate from one another but integrated.

- ❑ Emotional well-being has direct effects on physical well-being. Cardiovascular disease and cancer, in particular, are associated with fear, lack of courage or hope, and depression. We know, intuitively, that our emotional state affects how we feel, perform and has an impact on our overall health.

- ❑ I have seen, personally, how patients who reduced their stress lowered their blood pressure, became more engaged and productive at work, and found it easier to diet and exercise.

- ❑ At the medical school where I teach, we tell stories to help medical students "grow" their empathy. Surveys consistently show—unsurprisingly—that patients feel greater hope and have better outcomes when they feel their physician has listened to their story.[9]

Emotional energy, then, is vital to better overall health. So is spiritual energy. Evidence accumulates that people who are connected to family and friends and communities have better health outcomes, as do those whose lives are full of purpose.[10] Furthermore, the corporate athlete solution insists that the individual makes certain that his or her core values align with his or her entire range of behaviors, and vice versa. The corporate athlete solution asks the same of management: Is what the organization claims to believe actually aligned with how it acts? If the answer is yes, then the organization will certainly thrive.

It is not enough, then, to possess physical energy, even if there are large amounts of high-quality energy. One must be physically fit *and* emotionally connected, mentally focused and spiritually aligned. The integrated, comprehensive "four-in-one" approach of the corporate athlete solution is the key to its unique power; the key to its ability, ultimately, to succeed where others fail.

Can the corporate athlete solution be the start of the answer to our national healthcare crisis? Let's see: It leads to improved health; it has the potential to reach large populations of workers through corporate incentive-driven, employer-sponsored health insurance and wellness plans, as well as corporate-sponsored, community-based programs; and data confirms the positive ROI that organizations realize even when using programs far less well-rounded and persuasive than the corporate athlete solution.

An employee who is fully engaged—on *and/or* off work—is a highly productive, fulfilled employee and tends to be healthier. A healthy employee requires less healthcare than those sick. Turn enough employees—say, millions and millions?—who were once less healthy to being genuinely healthy, and our overall healthcare cost goes down. Way down. We all will benefit. That's precisely what the corporate athlete solution can deliver.

Chapter 6

Safe at Home and Beyond

by Alan McMillan

To whom does it mostly fall to ensure the safety and health of the employee? The organization? The government? The employee? What about when he or she is off the job? Is it completely up to the individual? Might it make sense for business to get involved there, too?

Workplace safety is no longer just about reducing injuries and accidents. These days it means dealing with escalating healthcare costs, dramatic shifts in workforce demographics, and the ever-present risks of global terrorism, devastating natural disasters or industrial accidents. Corporate safety and health programs are increasingly about saving businesses *and* lives. Businesses endeavor to address the demands of a new era by expanding safety and health programs beyond their traditional levels.

While I am pleased to say that America has experienced a steady decline in workplace deaths since 1992, America has, however, witnessed a 30-percent increase in preventable deaths in our homes and communities. Nine out of ten fatalities and nearly two-thirds of disabling injuries to workers occur off the job. If, for our purposes here, you will set aside the obviously devastating human cost of this loss, the financial cost is considerable. Employee injuries sustained on the job cost industries US$130 billion, while off-the-job injuries far surpass it, at US$200 billion. In 2005, U.S. employers lost 80 million days of production time to on-the-job injuries; off-the-job injuries cost industries more than twice as many lost days, at 195 million.[1]

As CEO of the National Safety Council (NSC), I appreciate that solutions to problems in the workplace are often to be found *beyond* the workplace, and resonate beyond the workplace, too. When I learned of the team from the Human Performance Institute, I was delighted to find innovators focused on helping to create safer, healthier environments for the 21st Century workforce. What I *hadn't* expected were the fundamental truths they unearthed—namely, that before I worked to remedy the problems plaguing other organizations, I first had to be willing to look at our own issues, at how we did things, and then at myself.

Once we looked in the mirror, the changes we—and I—aspired to make would be that much more powerful and enduring.

At a Leadership Summit in 2005, I heard Dr. Jack Groppel talk about the *power of full engagement* and how we all possess basic building blocks that can be developed to help us weather life's inevitable storms. Listening to Jack, I understood that one's "personal energy," and how one grows and manages it, is arguably the single greatest indicator of life success. I began to see the harsh, potentially tragic—yes, tragic—implications of multitasking, which in the short run can negate our ability to engage fully in any particular task at hand, and in the long run can erode our ability to summon sustained focus on the things that matter most.

I also understood how everyone, from Type A to Type Z, must have proper rest and recovery. Jack's talk invigorated me to work on enhancing my own store of physical energy, which, in turn, would help fuel my mental, emotional and spiritual energy. I began to question my *old story* and the ways in which it didn't support me (or even held me back). I grew excited about "writing" a thoroughly engaging, realistic *new story*, and the difference I could make in my work by living the new one. But before I could make such a difference, as I said above, I first needed to assess our organization.

We had just completed an "internal climate" survey at the National Safety Council to assess our 300+ employees' opinions about their work environment and elicit their input on potential improvements. Among the comments we received, a significant number talked about priorities such as recognition, value, expectations and balancing the many challenges that life continually offers. Given that my organization's *raison d'être* is to help organizations and communities become safer places to work and live, it struck me as vital to transform the Council into a better place to work, a great place to work. It was clear to me that the principles that comprised what Jack Groppel and his team called the *Corporate Athlete Advantage* would help us at the NSC to do that.

First, I realized that—on the job or off—humans are not work machines. We are *life* machines. The distinction could not be more profound. Companies should seek to maximize the "whole life" of a person, not just the "work-life." If we help build powerful people, they will build powerful organizations.

As CEO of a national non-profit organization devoted to improving work and living conditions, I needed to support my people in becoming more powerfully engaged not just at work but in *all* aspects of their lives—with their families, their emotional and physical health, their communities.

That is if the corporate athlete solution was applied to our lives for the purpose of helping us in our work, it would further echo in, and improve, our off-the-job lives. And if we esteemed the energy management principles so much that we thought they could support our organization as a whole, then I had to believe that they would help me, individually.

After hearing Jack speak, I attended HPI's two-and-a-half-day course in Orlando. It exceeded my already considerable expectations. I was so charged up that I invited Jim Loehr, a riveting speaker, to address our next Board of Directors meeting. We also selected a team of NSC trainers to go through the Orlando course including the train-the-trainer program, so we could communicate the message to our entire staff.

Within three months, we had sponsored our first corporate athlete classes at the NSC headquarters. We now have corporate athlete sessions almost every other month—and will continue until every employee who desires has an opportunity to participate. We also support employees who have been through the program to continue integrating the principles into their day-to-day lives; we send periodic e-mails and personal notes to their homes. We follow the corporate athlete nutritional guidelines and provide healthy food and drink options in our vending areas. We have held one corporate athlete alumni gathering to provide on-going support and plan to offer more. In addition, we foresee extending the program to interested family members of NSC employees. Through informal, positive feedback and personal stories, we are already realizing greater employee engagement.

Indeed, for those of us at the National Safety Council, the *Corporate Athlete Advantage* is more than a program that helps you find greater balance, engagement and fulfillment; it actually forwards our mission mandate. At the core of our 1953 Congressional Charter is a call to "arouse the nation" and to reduce injury and illness.[2] And it's simply impossible for us to fulfill that mission if American workers are unaware of and uncommitted to becoming fully engaged in what they do on *and* off the job, and to growing and maintaining their store of physical energy—in short, everything preached in the corporate athlete solution.

Stress, at work and in life, is an important component of developing the capacity for full engagement. But if unmanaged, it can be as damaging as exposure to chemical and biological hazards.

This is not an exaggerated statement made to be provocative: Experts warn that, if unaddressed, workplace stress ultimately drains the energy required to sustain a competitive business advantage, leading to dire consequences for companies, even entire industries, certainly countless employees. Stress, unabated by recovery, can be the hidden trigger behind cardiovascular and musculoskeletal complications, obesity, depression and violence—all costly on- and off-the-job disorders.

Stress cannot be avoided, but it can prompt personal growth. Throughout a large swath of Corporate America, the problem is that little, if any, effort is made by businesses to teach their workers how to recover from stress so that they are ready to manage the next stress. The corporate athlete solution champions the idea that one *builds capacity through stress and recovery*. It is my belief that this process significantly reduces the risk of accident, injury and illness, both on and off the job.

Interestingly, HPI's contention that stress is a necessary force, even an asset, if one knows how to properly deal with it, means that the corporate athlete solution's five concepts of stress and recovery look remarkably similar to the typical five-point corporate plan...for emergency preparedness!

Emergency Preparedness Plan	Corporate Athlete Solution
1. A corporate emergency plan is only as effective as the information it's based on and the organization's implementation ability.	1. Full engagement.
2. A plan that assumes certain response capabilities without practice or training will not be effective.	2. Train yourself and others.
3. Assess problems; response planning.	3. Build capacity.
4. Recovery: emergency operations, loss mitigation, how to continue operating under challenging circumstances.	4. Balance stress and recovery.
5. Fulfill corporate and professional mission.	5. Cultivate spirituality; life mission.

How central is the ability to deal with stress to creating a healthier and safer workplace environment? Nearly 70 percent of respondents to a 2006 Pew Research Center survey said that job stress is worse than it was a decade ago. Two of five view their work as "very" or "extremely" stressful. Expert estimates I have heard on the financial impact on businesses from costs attributed to stress such as stress-related accidents, illnesses, absenteeism, diminished productivity, mistakes, turnover and increased health insurance premiums, range from US$80 billion to US$150 billion annually.[3]

So how do we deal with this? Especially when the global business environment grows ever more competitive, not less?

In addition to stress, dramatic shifts in American demographics are another factor that's confounding safety and health in the workplace. First, our workforce is aging. The 55- to 64-year-old age group is growing at four times the rate of the total labor force.[4] While this age group actually has a lower percentage of injuries and illnesses than younger workers, when individuals *do* get injured or ill at work, they require additional time away from work[5] and their disabilities are more serious, which means higher workers' compensation costs. Also, aging workers are being replaced by younger workers with limited safety and health training or experience. Training the new generation of workers in proper safety and health practices is especially challenging because they are far more mobile than their predecessors. The average U.S. worker now changes jobs nine times before age 34. One-third of the total workforce changes jobs every year.[6]

Second, there is an increase in immigrant workers, most of whom are employed in high-injury occupations like construction, agriculture and transportation. The Hispanic population is the fastest growing ethnic group of the U.S. workforce,[4] so occupational safety and health training is more difficult because of language differences and cultural barriers, and, at times, literacy and education levels.

Third, more businesses are becoming multi-national, which means more businesses are struggling to establish consistency between and among multiple governments and their varying occupational safety and health standards.

So how does business deal with all these new challenges? The corporate athlete program offers one solution. Its principles are fundamental and far-reaching; it addresses problems experienced by corporate workers, yet it fully confronts how often these problems can also have their source off the job, away from the office.

Just as a wide range of individuals and industries and professions—from athletics to medicine to crime-fighting to national defense—use the corporate athlete solution to spur greater success, so today's safety and health professionals, and the executives who lead them, would be wise to follow its principles.

Fortunately, more businesses are discovering that focusing on employee safety and health positively influences both workforce morale and the bottom line. Outstanding leaders, whom I call CEOs who "get it," are starting to see employee safety/health and profitability as complementary; indeed, it's not dissimilar to how they have found the connection between corporate social responsibility and corporate fiscal health. These enlightened employers understand that employee safety and health are absolute keys to a productive workforce: It pays tremendous dividends in lower workers' compensation and insurance costs, as well as in improved employee productivity, morale and retention.

Employers are recognizing that as they better address and prevent both occupational and personal injury, illness and stress, they make their workers and their businesses safer and healthier—therefore more productive. Studies show that even modest efforts to carry the principles of workplace safety and health to employees' homes and communities reduce costs while also nurturing a more satisfied, motivated, productive workforce.

The outstanding leader, in my opinion, realizes that an effective safety and health program must have a core commitment from leadership to improve the corporate culture. Cultivate belief in the benefits of a safety and health culture and the barriers to employee buy-in start to dissipate. Promote such a culture and employees feel valued. They are more inclined to create quality products, to work harder, and do so in a way that's safer and healthier. Conversely, workers who don't embrace a culture of safety and health have a negative impact on quality, production and profitability. An organization benefits when management helps employees understand that their own well-being, and that of their families, is aided by adopting and practicing safe and healthy behaviors both on and off the job. In short, management sends the message that they care.

Sometimes management may need a timely reminder. In 2004, the National Institute for Occupational Safety and Health (NIOSH) introduced "Steps for a Healthier U.S. Workforce," a comprehensive plan to protect worker safety and health better than did traditional, fragmented strategies. By taking a more integrated approach, by aspiring to go so far as to identify and reduce factors that contribute to employee disease, disability and premature death, the NIOSH initiative represented a complete change for how organizations have acted and thought.

Clearly, the NIOSH was onto something. Since the program began, more and more businesses have expanded beyond "old school" compliance and accident prevention programs to address "radical" concepts—that is, if one regards concepts like health, wellness, stress and productivity management to be radical. Slowly but inexorably, businesses across the globe are eliminating their old story—namely, that safety and health, both on the job *and* off, are secondary and exclusively the domain of the organization's safety department. Increasingly, management views the safety and health of its workforce as a strategic business objective—and it should. It's in this way that organizations and their people will survive and prosper. It is in this way that organizations and their people will thrive.

But creating a safe and healthy environment is a responsibility that must be shared throughout the organization; the safety and health culture is ultimately the sum of each employee's story. It's good and well for management to provide employees with the knowledge, skills, training and motivation to minimize their risk of injury and to maximize benefits to their health, but the employee must fully embrace this mindset if it's to stick and become a corporate culture.

It still comes down to the individual. No one, after all, knows the employee's job better than he or she. No one sees the risks and problems inherent in that job as early or precisely. As much as the organization may want to overhaul the corporate culture, as much as we at NSC are engaged in trying to support improvement, in fact, it's a pretty tough thing. Because *you have to do it yourself.*

To be productive, you have to eat food that fuels you in the correct way. You have to exercise and move, in small and large ways, regularly. You have to include rest and recovery in your schedule and nurture your emotional and spiritual health. (Saying "it's impossible" is neither an option nor accurate.)

This is where I find the corporate athlete solution amazingly on point. It speaks to those in management about the need to lead and support an improved culture; yet it speaks also to the individual employee, and it recognizes that ultimately, for sustainable change to take place, the individual employee must understand and embrace new behaviors. Then incredible things will happen.

Let's briefly take a look at how the corporate athlete program addresses the global epidemic of stress without recovery.

As I stated earlier, stress, by itself, is not a bad thing. It's unavoidable, yes, it's challenging, yes, but it's also through stress that one changes and grows. However, a constant diet of stress can debilitate and lead to illnesses, if not death. So it's essential to find ways to recover from the inevitable, periodic, frequent stresses at work and at home. Indeed, the smartest organizations and employees prepare for stress—economic, natural and competitive storms—but do they build in recovery from stress? Once they have navigated through a crisis, then what? Stress—more accurately, stress without recovery—manifests itself as fatigue, anger, moodiness, even changes in appetite. It leads to distraction or lack of focus, which in turn may lead to an increase in accidents and mistakes. That means a greater likelihood of on- and off-the-job accidents, injuries and illnesses.

The corporate athlete solution encourages *strategic disengagement* to offset this major corporate problem. No reasonable person—not your colleagues, not your boss, not your family and, most of all, not yourself—could possibly deny the following fundamentals:

- ❑ Your body cannot spend more energy than it has.
- ❑ Human beings, as all living things, work best when they oscillate between periods of energy intensity and rest.
- ❑ If something is important enough to you (exercise, attending your child's after-school play, pursuing a passion), you can make it happen.
- ❑ To go through life without addressing how you feel, or if you can feel better, or how you might accomplish change, is completely unrealistic.

The corporate athlete solution, I discovered, is much more than just another way to make work-life safer and healthier. It is a solution to the basic problem of life.

Corporate America has made great progress in reducing workplace injuries and deaths and improving overall safety and health conditions for employees. The workplace injury-related death rate has declined 92 percent since the National Safety Council's founding in 1913. This reduction is especially significant given that, since the past century, the American workforce is quadruple the size and produces nine times the goods and services.[1]

I suggest that we can and will do better as employers recognize that a healthy business can develop and be sustained only when there is a healthy, well-rested, focused workforce. More and more are sponsoring stress management programs such as courses in yoga, time management, meditation and relaxation, to address and prevent stress in the workplace.

We have also seen more and more safety/health professionals promoted to senior positions at leading corporations. Presumably, these men and women are especially attuned to the need for their companies to support programs that help the worker maintain a better balance of his or her physical, emotional, mental and spiritual energy. Without balance, individuals suffer. Which means performance suffers. And ultimately business suffers.

One cannot remake a corporate culture overnight. For many organizations, the road from merely complying with basic standards to implementing innovative ideas and programs (and then continually assessing if and how well they work) can take years. Ultimately, to institute a new, better culture depends on commitment from corporate management and leadership, on employee engagement, on measurement and on continuous improvement. The transition from compliance and mere rules to seeing safety and health as ingrained corporate values, parallels the corporate athlete solution's concept of moving from *negative* to *positive* energy. Employees must consistently see the *new* principles in action. As they see the new principles being used more than the old ones, their attitudes and behaviors start to change. Eventually, the culture changes. A new story emerges.

Finally, when safety and health become values, they are instinctive to the entire organization. They underpin the beliefs, attitudes, values and principles that guide the business. They are sustained by policies, practices and procedures. When an organization achieves a true culture of safety and health, practices become habits and routine—or, using the terminology of the corporate athlete solution, *rituals*.

The principles of the corporate athlete solution are intuitive and rational. Ultimately, they are profound and life-affirming. They go hand in hand with corporate efforts to educate, train and motivate employees to embrace a culture of safety and health in all aspects of their lives.

Chapter 7

The Corporate Athlete Solution for Chief Learning Officers: The Calculus of Commitment

by Fred Harburg

It has been my honor to serve as the Chief Learning Officer (CLO) for some of the world's finest companies. As a CLO my departments were responsible for designing, delivering, purchasing, and managing leadership and organizational development programs. My experiences taught me that effective growth and change programs must have four characteristics: *They must be intensely personal, deeply meaningful, highly relevant and strongly supported by an embracing culture;* otherwise they are a monumental waste of time. When CLOs help create the right conditions for change, with an approach like that presented in the corporate athlete solution, the consequence is a significant return on engagement, productivity and overall business results. This approach provides a powerfully effective resolution of the engagement crisis that threatens our organizations, our society and our way of life.

> "There is a war for talent. Demand for leadership exceeds supply. From 1998 to 2008, while the workforce is expected to grow by 12 percent, the number of 25- to 44-year-olds from which tomorrow's leadership cadre will come, is expected to decline by 6 percent. This is true in North

America, Europe and parts of Asia."

—Michaels, E., Handfield-Jones, H. and Axelrod, B. (2001).
The War for Talent. Boston: Harvard Business School Press.

The Problem

Most business leaders readily acknowledge that the corporate world has an engagement problem. In actuality, research studies such as the Gallup findings which show that only 25 percent of workers are fully engaged, significantly understate the issue. There is an even more ominous storm on the horizon. As baby boomers begin to retire and the next generation of young professionals arrive, they view the work situation they are inheriting and shake their heads in dismay. In the frequent opportunities I have to speak to these promising young stars, they tell me that they see senior people buckling under a relentless work load. They observe escalating requirements for workplace activity outpacing the diminishing human energy supply required to fulfill demands. They note a retiring workforce that is in poor physical health despite an unprecedented media, marketing, and advertising blitz aimed at personal health and beauty. They witness older workers who have sacrificed their families and friendships on the altar of career "success." They watch people who lack enthusiasm for work or life because they have opted for money rather than balance. They see the fragmented lives of people who have tried to tune into ten channels of business activity simultaneously and focused on none of them fully. They notice people who are leaving careers of prominence to play golf each day with hollow and frustrating results. This next generation of leaders is carefully observing those who preceded them and are now reaching retirement age. These retirees have toiled for years but seem unfulfilled by their professional and personal lives. The observers see the finished product of decades of personal neglect, they perceive an unhealthy discrepancy between what they want and what they see and in response sing loudly, "Not for me!" The result is a lack of commitment, apprehension of the future, hesitancy to become engaged and withholding of discretionary effort. Young, high potential employees recognize that working harder is not necessarily smarter, desirable or sustainable. The next generation of workers thinks that there must be a better way but is not sure what it is.

> "Seventy-five percent of executives say they have weaknesses in their leaders' ability to meet the critical business challenges facing their company today. Two-thirds recognize significant weaknesses."
>
> —Mercer Delta Executive Learning Centers Leadership Imperative (GLI). (2006).

Overstated? I don't think so! Do your own research. Get the young people who have been identified to take the reigns of leadership in the next five to ten years in your organization to speak candidly and witness their lack of enthusiasm for the example set by their elders.

> "CEOs (66 percent) versus Board members (27 percent) report an 'excellent' level of assurance that the right leaders 'below the CEO' are in place."
>
> —Mercer Delta Study on Best Practices of Growth Companies. (2005).

The disenchantment manifests itself in two ways. First, the most talented people simply quit because they see no compelling reason to stay. All things being equal, employees will go where they get a better offer and the hope (often the myth) that conditions will be better in the new situation. The second manifestation appears in those who stay but quietly retire on active duty. They do only what they must to stay just above the line of acceptability. These "coasters" continually gauge what is required and identify how to keep a safe margin above the minimum to keep their jobs. They don't cause waves. They keep their heads down. They play the game not to lose. We have their bodies but *not* their hearts, their genius, their enthusiasm or their full engagement.

The good news is that this problem is actually a remarkable opportunity in disguise. Organizations that create the conditions for full engagement of their talent have an enormous advantage over the competition. As a senior business leader you have both the obligation and the opportunity to create an organization of vibrantly engaged workers. I have personally experienced this kind of environment several times in my career. At the ROLM Corporation (the digital telephone equipment company that was purchased by IBM and became one of its wholly owned subsidiaries), for instance, the energetic and intelligent efforts of employees spun like an electromagnet creating a winsome force that attracted other talented people: Our business performance and results soared. At another of the companies which I was privileged to work for, the Saturn Corporation, we also created the type of energy that allowed us to attract and retain the best of the best at a time when there was indeed a tug-of-war for talent. The next generation of workers knows they want to play on that kind of team.

The Benefits of a New Game

What does this old game of disengagement cost and what value would emerge if we were to solve this problem? To calculate the benefits of a new game you must differentiate between the current level of engagement in your organization and the level that is possible. The CEO of one of the world's largest and most profitable businesses once commented to me, "The only thing that limits our company from taking advantage of existing and new business opportunities is our shortage of qualified, fully engaged leaders." Senior executives across the full spectrum of industries resonate with this statement and its many implications.

There is increasing recognition that one of the primary jobs of a senior leader is to continually raise the performance capability of organizational talent in a way that is consistent with its mission and values. This realization is creating a merger of roles between the Chief Learning Officers and Chief Talent Officers. The world's leading organizations are beginning to measure a CLO's success by examining the extent to which he or she closes the engagement gap in the high potential talent pool. Successful development efforts can be gauged by examining the slope of the performance capability growth curve. If the slope of your curve is sharper and more sustained than that of the competition, you will inevitably win the race; if it is not, you will suffer the consequences. It is the same for an Olympic athlete. At any specific moment in the buildup to an athletic competition, the question is what is the slope of the performance growth curve relative to the targeted performance objectives and how steady and sustained is the growth? In many ways this is pure physics, and it begs that we observe the indisputable laws of energy management. If we violate these laws, we suffer; if we observe and harness them, we prosper. In this new game, what's at stake is nothing short of our viability to compete and win.

"Issues of leadership talent and employee engagement were identified to be among primary CEO concerns...Over 4,500 leaders from around the world cited improving and leveraging talent as their second business priority on a list of 14, preceded only by improving customer service relationships."

—Bernthal, P.R. and Wellins, R.S. (2005). *Leadership Forecast 2005-2006: Best Practices for Tomorrow's Global Leaders.*

Intensely Personal

The first requirement for an effective development process is that it be intensely personal if it is to make a real difference. Change is inevitable. Customers change their expectations and tastes. Competition becomes fiercer. Competitors change what they are doing in an attempt to take your market from you. Employees retire or move on and new ones join the organiztion. Economic factors such as interest rates, currency values, the money supply and consumer spending all change. The political and international landscape of interdependencies, alliances and conflicts turns upside down and inside out. Federal regulations and standards change. Technology is transforming entire industries and morphing the way we work, play, learn and buy things. We simply can't escape it—there has never been a time of such rapid and dramatic change. Although change is inescapable, growth is a choice followed by a lot of hard work. And if the benefits of change become personal and positive, it is work that pays big dividends.

In an attempt to be competitive, businesses change, restructure, reorganize, merge, acquire, divest, struggle to turn around and attempt to renew their culture. All of these efforts are aimed at increasing organizational viability. More often than not these efforts fall short and fail to hit the mark. The question is why and what can we do to create a highly desirable future? A significant part of the answer lies in the fundamental logic upon which successful change depends. Most mergers, reorganizations, restructurings and culture change efforts remain impersonal abstractions that are communicated to people in slickly spun corporate newsletters and streaming video. Rather than enrolling people to support the change with enthusiasm, these programs often engender tremendous resistance and resentment. In contrast, when we see organizations or individuals that thrive in the face of intense challenge they make the change real, practical and very personal by doing three things that lie at the core of the corporate athlete solution:

- ❏ First, they clearly *face the truth* about the current situation and how they got there.
- ❏ Second, they compellingly *define the purpose* they are striving to achieve.
- ❏ Finally, they consistently *take action* that will make their purpose a reality, and they cease actions and behaviors that are working against them.

These three steps are not an abstract academic theory, nor are they an esoteric model of change; rather they are a plain statement of fact about our observation of thousands of people who have made remarkable changes. These steps are just as true for an organization as they are for an individual, and they are the foundation of the corporate athlete solution.

Let me provide you with a brief illustration from my experience. I spent several years as a U.S. Air Force officer and pilot. Experience taught me that there is one thing a pilot has to know and continually update during a flight—his or her current position and situation relative to the mission objectives. It's crucial for a pilot to know the accurate facts about where the plane is, where the enemy is, how much fuel remains, the burn rate, what the weather is doing to the trajectory, and the current condition and capability of the aircraft and the crew. It's also important for the pilot to understand how they got into the current situation, particularly if they need to change course. If the airplane is stalling, spinning or sputtering it is imperative to understand what happened to create this condition so we can take the action required to correct it and complete the mission.

Because all of this information is complex and is constantly changing, it is easy to get it wrong. The pilot has to ensure that the information is reliable and accurate. At times pilots strongly, but wrongly, believe their plane is turning upside down even when the instruments are telling them that the plane is straight and level—this condition is called vertigo. When a pilot follows an inaccurate instinct and fails to verify that the instruments are correct, they will die.

It is no less important for you as a CLO to help leaders in your business gain an accurate assessment of their current position. On the grand scale of the business this means asking questions like the following:

- ❑ Where are we with respect to products and services that our customers want and will pay for?
- ❑ Where do we stand with respect to achieving superior quality standards at a cost that makes us strongly competitive?
- ❑ How are we progressing with respect to global competitors, global opportunities and global markets?
- ❑ How are we progressing toward retaining and fully engaging the most talented people in our industry?

On a more personal level:

- ❑ What is the level of enthusiasm I have for my current role?
- ❑ Do I have the physical energy and mental focus required to consistently perform at the highest levels of excellence?
- ❑ Does my weight and blood chemistry data indicate that I am at a healthy level to face the continuing demands of my job?
- ❑ Do I have a compelling personal purpose that sustains me in the face of significant challenges?
- ❑ Do I have a set of adaptive emotional routines that help me maintain equilibrium and connect with others in a fulfilling way?
- ❑ Am I growing my knowledge and mental capabilities to be at the top of my professional game?
- ❑ Am I consistently making strategic recovery a part of my daily routine so I can be fully engaged in my professional and personal endeavors?

These are questions that help you establish your current position and they require you to tell the sometimes painful truth. Learning from your personal history about the key events, decisions, beliefs, actions, habits and stories that propelled you into this position can help you take effective corrective action to achieve your desired objectives and purpose. If the information about your current situation is *inaccurate* or *based on an unwillingness or inability to face the truth squarely*, you base your actions on false premises and, like the vertigo pilot, the consequence can be devastating.

Ultimately, if positive change is to take place in an organization, it must be personal. It has been my pleasure to work with many of our corporate athletes in making a very personal application of these fundamental truths regarding change. I recently received a letter from the country President of a multinational pharmaceutical company who after one of our corporate athlete programs reversed a decade-long problem with his blood chemistry and, even more importantly, turned around an erosion of his family and work situations because he chose to courageously face the truth and to take corrective action. He is ecstatic and so are his co-workers and his family.

Deeply Meaningful

The second rule for effective organizational change is that it must be deeply meaningful if it is to make a significant and lasting difference. Many of today's workers experience their jobs as an endless marathon going nowhere. They conclude that their employers don't really care about them. They find little meaning in their work other than to get a paycheck. They perceive little if any loyalty from the organization and in return they feel none to it. We are truly in an era of free agency. What is true for the present generation of workers is even more so for the next. According to Dr. Ken Dychtwald, author of *Age Wave*,[1] the next generation of workers has looked at the current situation and decided not to buy in. They are uninspired by the lifestyle and tradeoffs of the current employment contract.

> "…Companies with stronger leadership development systems enjoy higher returns on equity in profit when compared with their competitors."
> —Bernthal, P.R. and Wellins, R.S. (2005).
> *Leadership Forecast 2005-2006: Best Practices for Tomorrow's Global Leaders.*

In their recent book, *How to Beat the Coming Shortage of Skills and Talent*, Ken Dychtwald along with co-authors Tamara Erickson and Robert Morison warn leaders that they must make a new deal with workers if they hope to engage them in a meaningful way.[2] In addition to the ideas these authors express regarding the physical, financial, time and contextual dimensions of work, my professional experiences and personal observations lead me to conclude that one of the most important solutions to the current epidemic of disengagement lies in changing the relationship between a leader and those led. Managers who consistently demonstrate interest and respect for others, and who demonstrate an ability to evoke superior sustained performance by providing effective coaching, enjoy a tremendous business advantage over those who lack this competence.

> "The vast majority of top financial performing companies (85 percent of the top 20 in a field of 373 companies) hold managers accountable for developing talent, compared to just 46 percent of leaders from other organizations."
>
> —*How the Top 20 Companies Grow Great Leaders.* (2005). Lincolnshire: Hewitt Associates.

This begins for corporate athletes by helping them find a compelling sense of purpose and direction in their work. At the top of the energy pyramid is the spiritual. By spiritual we don't necessarily mean religious, though for some it may. Having a strong spiritual point on the pyramid means having a very personal, values-based answer to the question, "What is the ultimate purpose I am pursuing that is more important than any temporary setback or hardship?" It is our observation that hardships and storms are an inevitable part of the landscape and that only when an individual or a group has a compelling sense of purpose and direction are they able to weather significant storms.

After four years of effort to start up the Saturn Corporation, it seemed that the obstacles were insurmountable. It was not merely our foreign competitors that created challenge for us; the other car divisions of our own parent company expressed significant resistance to our success. In addition, the complexity of starting a new company while simultaneously designing a series of new vehicles was overwhelming. There were many times in the early years when we gathered collectively as a leadership team to hear the news that our continued funding was questionable and that our company was at risk. In the midst of this, we all felt that what we were doing had a noble purpose. We genuinely understood that consumers deserved a better purchasing and ownership experience than was available with the average automotive company. We also realized a deep sense of commitment to demonstrating that an American manufacturing company was still viable in a global market place where "Made in America" was a slogan with dwindling cachet. What we were attempting seemed deeply important to our country and to future generations of American workers and consumers. This sense of purpose was deeply meaningful and it sustained us in the midst of terrific storms that raged around us.

As a CLO you have the opportunity to help your business and the individuals in it find a sense of purpose that will inspire workers to train harder and achieve higher levels of commitment and engagement. Corporate athletes who thrive find deep meaning in both a personal and organizational context.

Highly Relevant

The third organizational change rule is this; to be effective, change must be highly relevant. The change must be embodied in practical aspects of daily activity. For the corporate athlete we call this the power of ritual. The translation from goals to results occurs through consistent actions carefully chosen to achieve the milestones on the road to success. Dr. Jack Welch of General Electric fame called this the power of an operating routine. When he was in pursuit of a goal that he called organizational "boundarylessness,"[3] he instilled a set of powerful operating routines related to sharing information across organizational boundaries. It quickly became a frequent ritual for every business head to send invitations to their peers to see innovations, new ideas and best practices that were working outside the bounds of their own businesses. This is how Jack expressed it in the 1994 General Electric (GE) annual report:

> "Boundaryless behavior has become the 'right' behavior at GE. Since the early 1980s, as the company downsized in order to become more globally competitive, we often heard the question, 'How much more can be squeezed from the lemon?' *This zero-sum-thinking did not foresee the immense reservoir of creativity and energy that flows from an engaged workforce that increasingly embraces three fundamental operating behaviors.*

We have described these three behaviors in past letters: boundarylessness, speed and stretch. They have evolved from philosophical, 'soft' concepts into behaviors that deliver hard results, and they are the reason for both today's success and the enormous potential we see for tomorrow."

Jack Welsh went on to describe how this soft concept (bound-arylessness) had delivered top- and bottom-line results by spreading best practices across the borders of GE and becoming operating routines with the following examples:

❏ "Demand Flow Technology" to double and triple in-ventory turn rates.

❏ "Bullet Train Thinking" to take 30 to 50 percent out of product costs over a two-year period.

❏ "Quick Market Intelligence," the weekly direct cus-tomer feedback technique.

❏ "Half-Movement"—half the parts, half the weight, in half the time.

He concluded:

"Boundaryless behavior has become the 'right' behavior at GE and aligned with this behavior is a rewards system that recognizes the adapter or implementer of an idea as much as its originator."

By moving purpose, goals and objectives to specific actions that become rituals, corporate athletes make change highly relevant and highly productive for all. As a CLO you have the opportunity to fur-ther personalize the power of operating routine by helping the tal-ented people in your organization identify highly relevant personal rituals that they will resonate with and grow their personal energy reserves.

Strongly Supported By an Embracing Culture

The final rule for effecting positive change involves CEO partnership in the creation of a culture of high commitment and high energy. Multiple studies indicate that the most crucial issue for the success of a change effort is the active support of senior leadership.

Imagine for a moment that you worked for a CEO who thought

that the key to organizational effectiveness and financial viability of the company is determined by the extent to which the people of the organization are able to access and continually cultivate deeper sources of personal and professional energy. If you work for P&G, your dream just came true. A.G. Lafley, Chairman, President and CEO of Procter & Gamble, is one of a number of forward thinking leaders who have embraced the task of reshaping a corporate culture to support the full engagement of its people. His personal example as well as his genuine investment in making every employee at P&G a high performing, high energy corporate athlete is a resounding affirmation of this solution.

It is hard to overemphasize the importance of an embracing culture. If there is a contest between a strong system and a strong individual, the system will win almost every time. As a CLO one of your primary objectives in implementation of the corporate athlete solution must be to fully enroll your CEO and to help him or her be both the owner and the exemplar of the change.

I briefly mentioned ROLM Corporation earlier. Let me further elaborate the ROLM culture and leadership so you can better understand the power of an embracing culture. In the early 1970s, when the digital telecommunication revolution was just dawning, ROLM was a tiny player with a huge belief in the power of fully engaged people. The company set out to make its mark as a small start-up business in a field that was massively dominated by AT&T. Northern Telecom was the only other major player in the North American phone switching business.

When the four founders of ROLM established a permanent campus in Santa Clara, California, among the first buildings they funded was a huge co-educational gymnasium, featuring a swimming complex, tennis courts and fitness center surrounded by beautiful running trails and exercise stations. More than two-thirds of the employees regularly used the facilities. This was a phenomenon even for California. It made a huge statement about who we were and what we stood for. In addition to the fitness facilities was a gourmet dining facility in which ROLM employees could find delicious, healthy food choices that were heavily subsidized by the company. Of course employees could also find grease burgers, but these were taxed rather than subsidized to help defray the costs of healthy choices. These features brought to life an embracing culture for maximizing employee engagement.

ROLM also took the idea of strategic recovery very seriously. To keep workers intellectually fresh, we gave each employee three months of paid time off for every six years of service. So, when people returned from a short stint in the Peace Corps or from helping with an archeological dig in Northern Africa, for example, they brought back a fresh attitude and new energy for approaching intractable problems.

This sort of culture made ROLM a talent magnet and the business success sensation of the age. We were able to freely attract the best talent from companies like Apple and Hewlett Packard. We drew the finest young minds from Stanford, Massachusetts Institute of Technology and California Institute of Technology. Before we were purchased by IBM at the peak of a remarkable set of business results achievements, it was my privilege to replicate this environment in Colorado Springs at ROLM's newest facility. There in the foothills of the Rockies I hired the first corporate fitness director and built the first corporate fitness complex of significant size in the Pike's Peak region. This was not merely a recruiting strategy, it was an engagement approach. When I recently spoke with a colleague who had been the ROLM general manager and business unit head in Colorado Springs, he talked about our partnership and the remarkable level of energy and engagement we were able to achieve on the way to extraordinary business results as a consequence of the innovative changes.

> "Between 1982 and 2003, the Brookings Institution found a dramatic shift in the percent of an average company's value that could be attributed to physical assets (i.e., equipment, facilities and other tangible physical assets) versus those that could be attributed to intangible assets (i.e., patents, intellectual property, brand and, most of all, people)."
>
> ❏   In 1982: 62% tangible, 38% intangible
>
> ❏   In 2003: 20% tangible, 80% intangible
>
> —Barrington, L. and Silvert, H. (2004).
> *CEO Challenge 2004: Top 10 Challenges.* The Conference Board.

Winning Commitment

In the face of the relentless changes businesses are encountering, we must find ways to have workers show up fully engaged to tackle the serious business challenges of our times. The examples of fully engaged work teams, like those I have cited here, offer a compelling value proposition for embracing an engagement strategy. As a senior business leader you have a unique and important opportunity to take the performance capability of your business to a new level. The tested approach to making positive change found in the corporate athlete solution is intensely personal, deeply meaningful, highly relevant and strongly supported by an embracing culture. When you use it you take a bold step toward resolving the engagement crisis and strengthening your organization, our society and a way of life.

Chapter 8

The Non-Athlete Corporate Athlete

by Jenny Evans

Perhaps you have never considered yourself an athlete. You have never excelled in sports, gym class was a nightmare and you were always the last one chosen for a game. Remember when the teacher selected team captains and then had everyone else line up against the gym wall? The same people were always chosen first. As the teams began to form, you tried to make eye contact with one of the captains. Your pleading look said, "You are one of my closest friends. *Surely* you will pick me next!"

At the Human Performance Institute, we work with professional and elite athletes from all over the world, military hostage rescue teams, law enforcement, medical and business professionals to expand their capacity to perform in high-stress arenas. Stories of how these performers overcame obstacles to become the best in the world in their discipline never fail to impress, inspire or awe.

But perhaps you cannot identify with winning the U.S. Open, or with completing a life-threatening mission (which many of our clients, from military elite Special Forces to Navy SEALs, must perform regularly). Maybe you have never dreamed of setting a world record, never had the desire to become number one in the world, never experienced that defining moment of physical greatness where, just as it looked as if you were about to fail, you rallied to triumph.

Me, neither.

As a young child, I was exceptionally clumsy. I had stitches in my head twice before the age of five. There should have been a third set of stitches, but my mother feared that if she took me to the emergency room again, the doctors might think I was an abused child. So nervous was my Mom about my physical well-being, she signed me up for dance classes, hoping I would develop some basic coordination and accomplish the feat of chewing gum and walking at the same time.

Part of my problem may have been my deformed hips, which caused me to be pigeon-toed: My feet turned in at about a 45-degree angle. To fix this structural deformity, I wore corrective shoes that came in two styles: ugly and uglier. My "clodhoppers." I also had to wear custom-made orthotics inside the shoes. These were the only shoes I was allowed to wear. No fun sneakers, no kicky Mary Janes.

Naturally, I came to regard gym class as torture—torture made more exquisite by the annual Presidential Physical Fitness contest, in which you had to run the 50-yard dash and shuttle run, perform the long jump, timed sit-ups and the bent arm hang (pull-ups, if you were a boy). To this day, I still don't understand the benefit of being able to hold your chin above a bar for an extended period of time. For my efforts every year, I was awarded the "I tried" ribbon. Thank you very much. I will hang this one in my room right next to the other six I already own...

In Junior High, I decided to go out for track. How hard could it be? All you had to do was run in a circle. There is no coordination needed for that. When I crossed the finish line, my coach didn't give me a time...he gave me a day of the week. I wish I were kidding.

At about this time, I contracted what the doctor diagnosed as "collagen disease," a condition in which one's collagen, a protein that helps make bones strong, becomes inflamed, swollen and quite painful. Whatever position I was in when I fell asleep was the position I would stay for the rest of the night; it was too painful to move. In the morning I had to warm up to be able to move. My feet hurt so much that even walking was sometimes unbearable. (Later, in my twenties, I was re-diagnosed with rheumatoid arthritis.)

While riding my bike the summer I was 16, I was struck by a car. The main injury was to my spine. And so began considerable back pain, immobility and years of visits to the physical therapist and chiropractor. It was during this time that doctors discovered I had scoliosis (an excessive curvature of the lumbar region of the spine).

I'm not sharing all these facts to elicit pity or to complain about my plight. So many people have serious limitations and injuries; compared to their situation, mine was relatively insignificant.

No, I share this to highlight the breathtaking number of stories I created around these facts and experiences, to justify each. I contend that it was not my injuries that made me a victim of circumstance; I was a victim of my circumstances because of the stories I told about my injuries, my clumsiness, my "obvious" lack of physical ability. In fact, I had an entire library of stories. Here is a short version of just one of them: "I am definitely *not* an athlete. I have many physical limitations that prevent me from excelling in sports, and in the big picture, sports are not important. What is important is to be good in school. All these guys are just inconsiderate, so it doesn't really matter if I'm always chosen second-to-last anyway."

Can you identify with any aspect of this story? If you are a supposed "non-athlete"—and I know you are out there, since I have worked with too many to count—then I suspect you *can* relate. Maybe you can't relate because you have always been gifted at sports and spent every spare moment playing...but perhaps there are other areas in your life (work, family, various unrealized dreams and pursuits) where a story like mine—seemingly logical and airtight—sounds alarmingly autobiographical.

In college, I majored in Psychology. I wanted to help people sort through their problems and find happiness and fulfillment in their lives. To cover my tuition, I needed another job besides waitressing. The University Recreational Center was looking for aerobic instructors. With my dance background, I thought it would be a great way to make money, continue to dance, have a chance to "perform" and, best of all, get paid to work out!

I fell in love with it. I saw the changes that occurred in me but also in others—especially the students who would sneak in at the last minute so that they would go unnoticed, finding a spot in the back of the room. Gradually, over the course of several weeks, they would move out of the back row. Soon they were coming early, in anticipation of their workout. Eventually they would walk in with shoulders back, head high, a look of confidence on their faces. They were different people, physically and emotionally. I was hooked.

I switched my major to Kinesiology. I was fascinated by how you could get the body to adapt and change if you just knew how to provide the right stimuli. While still in college, I started a personal and corporate fitness training company; part of my job was training executives one-on-one in their offices or homes. I also began to manage corporate wellness centers.

A byproduct of my job was that I was increasing my physical fitness. Teaching several types of fitness classes and working out with clients improved my cardiovascular endurance, muscular strength, flexibility and reduced my body fat. But I still didn't consider myself an athlete, just a fitness professional.

At the Human Performance Institute, we ask clients to identify the self-told stories that prevent them from accomplishing their life missions. For instance: What excuses do you make for not being engaged with your family after a long, exhausting day's work? How do you rationalize not having time to eat breakfast, or to exercise? How do the stories you tell yourself and others let you off the hook, so you can justify *not* doing the things that, deep down, you know you should and can accomplish?

We certainly receive some grand tales. These excuses come to be reframed as the client's *old story* (as we call it at HPI). After our clients write their old story, we guide them through a process to craft a *new story*, one that inspires them to make tough, values-based decisions about how to invest their energy in ways that allow them to become the extraordinary leaders, parents, spouses or family members—in short, the people—they know they *have and want* to be.

It's only natural that I would turn the mirror on myself. What stories did *I* regale myself with that were huge barriers? What did I tell myself that kept me from being the most fully realized person imaginable?

Since seventh grade I had told myself I wasn't a runner. "Not only am I terrible at running, it's incredibly boring, and all that jarring is really bad for my ailing joints." This story, I decided, had to go. After all, did I have the physical ability to run? Yes, I did.

Why did this story in particular need to be rewritten? In the grand scheme, it seemed pretty insignificant. What was the big deal? How could seeing myself as a runner make me a better performance coach, a better mother, a better daughter?

I place a lot of value on using my skills. Not just using them, but using all of them to their *full potential*. I still haven't identified my full potential, nor do I think I ever will, because I continue to experience growth in all aspects of my life—physically, emotionally, mentally and spiritually. I believe that not giving life to everything one has is a tragic waste of talent, skills and gifts.

To overcome our old stories and negative habits, we must establish positive rituals, which, when given extraordinary energy, begin to grow and crowd out our negative habits. If you put your arm in a cast, the muscles start to atrophy or shrink, due to lack of use, stimulus, exposure to stress and energy investment. Conversely, if you want a muscle to grow bigger, you must continually expose it to progressively more stress than what it's used to. Over time, the muscle becomes stronger and begins to hypertrophy or grow. So it's vital to start investing energy in what you want, not in what you don't want. When you are on a diet, what are you constantly thinking about? What you *can't* have. Clearly, I had to start growing some new "muscles."

Ritual #1: Stop giving energy to my old story about running.
Just stop. Cut off its energy supply. In the past, whenever a conversation turned to the topic of running, I would enthusiastically talk about how bad a runner I was, how much I hated it, how my body wasn't designed for it, how boring it was, how it could not be good for my back. But our stories, for better or worse, become our reality, and by continually telling this story, I gave energy to it. It grew bigger and stronger every year. In short: I made it real. All that would have to stop. Maybe I wasn't quite ready to say that I *wanted* to run, or that I loved running. But the first step was just to stop telling my old story, and thus cut off its blood supply.

Ritual #2: Put running on my calendar.
It was a commitment that had to be met, like it or not. It also gave me time to prepare for my running sessions. I would know exactly what days they were scheduled, so I could start mentally preparing for the run the day before. I would visualize myself running around the lake with good form and decent speed, feeling great, with no side aches.

Ritual #3: Pick a route and stick with it.
After a week of running to and around a lake in my neighborhood, I realized I was responsible only for running halfway around it. Why? Because there is only one way back home, and that's to get around the back side of the lake. (If I ran on the treadmill, on the other hand, I could take a shortcut anytime I wanted, just by hitting that bright, shiny, tempting "stop" button.)

Ritual #4: Pick great running music.
I had my challenge music with me, which could pump me up, energize me and pace me all the way home.

Ritual #5: Come up with new stories powerful enough to replace the old, tired ones, as soon as they popped into my head.
Our old stories are very powerful, of course—we have been telling them for years to anyone who would listen! Every time I ran, fragments of my old story would start to whisper, talk or even shout at me, depending on the day.

"What am I doing out here?...I'm not a runner...I think I'm dying..."

How could I get these stories out of my head? It wasn't easy. It's not easy for anyone. To prove it, try this exercise: Visualize the Eiffel Tower in as much detail as possible—color, height, time of day, the crowds...Got it? Now *stop* thinking about the Eiffel Tower. No matter what you do, do *not* think about the Eiffel Tower. Have you erased the Eiffel Tower from your mind? Seriously, stop picturing the Eiffel Tower!

Did you succeed in *not* thinking about the Eiffel Tower? The only way you could have succeeded was to replace the picture of the Eiffel Tower with something different. Obviously, I had to replace my ridiculous stories with something new.

While some of my new stories had taken time to create, many of the best ones I had come up with in a split second, in a moment of weakness, while in some significant physical discomfort. Spontaneous as they were, these stories—some profound, some silly—carried me through my weak moments. Here are just a few: "My worst day is someone else's best day...If something ever happened to my legs—God forbid—what would be the one thing I would fantasize about doing?...Breathe, flow, let it go...The Boogeyman is right behind you. And he is seriously about to grab you. His fingers are just an inch away...Fatigue is just a state of mind. Mind over matter. You can do it...If my daughter Isabella was struggling with something really difficult, would I encourage her to give up? Not in a million years. So just keep running...If I can make it through natural childbirth, I think I can make it three more blocks. So just run...If you have already gone this far, you can make it the rest of the way. So keep running...Keep running. Keep running!!!"

I began my training mission to become a runner on Monday, May 22nd, 2006. I ran a loop around my neighborhood, maybe 2 miles. I was disappointed with my performance. I had assumed it couldn't be all *that* hard—after all, I had been teaching fitness classes for years and had a good base—but my fitness level did not translate to running particularly well. Running was different; it called on other, previously unused muscle groups. I made it back to my house and tried to feel good at least about keeping my commitment and beginning my training mission.

My ritual was to run the same loop three times per week, while not timing myself or concerning myself with speed. All I needed was to get out the door and run. Over the weeks, my route gradually grew—yet it was still unbelievably difficult. I was constantly out of breath. I often got side aches. Many days it felt as if I had accidentally put on a heavier pair of legs.

Then, on Tuesday, June 13th, something happened: It was not my scheduled day to run...but I went for a run anyway. Can you believe it? Me, the non-runner, was now looking forward to a run! *Craving* a run! Ironically, I felt physically wretched during the entire run. But I still did it.

Gradually, I increased to running to Lake Nokomis, around it, and back home again—approximately 5 miles—without dying. I started to run more than three times a week, at times as many as five. I had days when I felt really strong, but there were still plenty of poor performances. I didn't let it stop me, though. I was on a mission.

After a little coaxing, I signed up for a 5K race with a friend. It was a big step for me, more mental than physical. The last time I had competed in a race was in seventh grade, a dismal failure. Only *runners* signed up for races. Was I really a runner? Or just a fitness professional pretending to be a runner?

The date was August 5th, 2006. I had been in training for 76 days.

At the race I looked at the people around me. At first, I noticed only those who looked like runners: serious, decked out in top-notch running gear, not shorts and a shirt like me. Were there other people there? You bet—plenty of people there just to have fun. But the ones who intimidated me, who made me doubt my place there, were the serious runners.

In the weeks leading up to the race, I had trained not just physically but mentally and emotionally as well. I decided to run the race for the fun of it. No pressure. It would be great time spent with my friend, and it would simply be my workout for the day. I reminded myself that I had run longer than 5K plenty of times. This would be a shorter run than what I was used to.

I took my spot at the back of the pack and tried to remember I was there for fun. The gun went off and the swarm of runners surged. My body felt good. I settled in to a mildly uncomfortable pace. Several people passed me. I passed a few people myself. Then I passed a few more. I finished the race knowing I had pushed myself as hard as I was capable. It was a fun experience, very unlike the running episodes I had endured two decades earlier on the running track.

Before that day, I had never before timed my runs, so I had no idea what kind of pace I ran. After cooling down, I went to look at the time postings, out of curiosity.

I was third in my age division.

No way.

I couldn't help but laugh. Jenny the non-runner, the non-athlete, had just won a medal. Not an "I tried" ribbon; a medal. I was finally convinced that I was a runner.

The next day, a thought popped into my head: What if only the really crappy runners signed up for that race? Maybe the race wasn't really that competitive.

"Hello, old story. I knew you would try to make a comeback. You have been subverting me for half my life."

Do you see how powerful our old stories are? It's amazing the hold they have on us. I knew I had been successful in my training mission, but I realized I needed to train to make it an undeniable success, one that could never again be doubted or second-guessed.

My friend and I decided to sign up for the Iron Girl Duathlon, which would take place in September. I have to admit what got me was "Iron Girl." I loved the humor in it—not an Ironman, an Iron Girl. The race consisted of a 2-mile run, a 22-mile bike ride and another 2-mile run. It was great to have a new goal and a training partner. My friend was a faster runner than I, but I could beat her on the bike. She would pull me and make me run as hard as I could, and I could return the favor on the biking leg. Having a new goal kept me consistent with my training, despite my heavy travel schedule for work. Did I really want to feel horrible for 26 miles? No thanks. Just keep running!

We finished in the top 10 percent of 500 women.

I continued to run over the winter, which in Minneapolis is a formidable feat. My rule: If it was 18 degrees or warmer, I was out running; if it was colder, I did yoga or put my bike on the trainer in the basement.

Why did I endure as I was being pelted with sideways-flying snow? Why did I get on the bike in our dark basement? Because I was clear on my mission: to use my skills to the best of my ability. To continually expand my capacity. To discover my limits, and then keep excelling.

In the spring I competed in another duathlon and took third place in my age division with a time of 1:29:31 hours. I was now the proud owner of *two* medals. I had several more to go before they outnumbered my "I tried" ribbons. But they would. Trust me, they would.

So...was I *now* an athlete?

That depends on how you define "athlete."

I realized that an "athlete" can be many different things. Often we define an athlete as someone who excels at popular sports like basketball, football, baseball, etc...But now I realized something. Just because in Junior High basketball I ran the wrong way and took a shot at the opponent's basket did not mean I wasn't an athlete. (Thank God my basketball skills were so awful that I missed the shot.) The fact that I never excelled at traditional sports did not mean I wasn't an athlete. Many of us need to redefine what "athlete" or "athletic" means and how it may encompass a variety of activities and aptitudes. For example, besides running, I also started to do the flying trapeze—something I first had an opportunity to try on a vacation at an all-inclusive resort; I got on the swing but could not make my body follow the instructor's pretty elementary commands (his voice couldn't hide his disgust when he told me finally to just get off the swing); then returned to it, fell in love with everything about it and began to master it. All the training—developing strength and control and fearlessness, along with the *full engagement* I experienced when I was in the midst of swinging and flying—couldn't that be called athletic?

To keep pushing my limits, I continue to train, adapt and integrate new rituals. Here are some of the rituals I have implemented to stay engaged, despite having a family, a career that requires me to travel roughly two to six times a month and no fitness club membership:

Physical:

- ❑ I work out five days a week. Although I'm frequently traveling, I always know at least a week in advance when I will travel. So if I'm traveling Tuesday through Thursday, I make Tuesday my off-day, exercise on Wednesday, and make Thursday my other off-day. Also, I'm flexible within the ritual of exercise itself: Depending on my schedule, it could be 2 hours on my road bike followed by 45 minutes of running…*or* the whole session might be just 10 minutes of stretching. But no matter what, I *never* skip my ritual. Skip just a few days and it's too easy to fall off the wagon and abandon the ritual altogether.

- ❑ I never go more than 4 hours without eating. I eat several small meals throughout the day to keep my energy levels up, my metabolism burning strong, my glucose levels steady; it keeps me from becoming what in my family we call "hangry"—hungry and angry. When I'm cranky and impatient, the first question my daughter asks is, "Do you need a snack?" When I travel, I keep food with me at all times. It's easy to keep my briefcase stocked with trail mix, energy bars and chocolate-covered peanuts. I will never let my performance or mood be out of my control. It's just too important.

- ❑ I remain hydrated by drinking moderate amounts of water all day and keeping caffeinated beverages to a minimum. I love my morning coffee—the smell, the taste, the little kick—but I have only two to three small cups. I used to have a diet cola every afternoon; I have recently vanquished that from my routine. My energy levels actually stay stronger through the late afternoon without caffeine. While I continue to love the "burn," I get my fix by drinking carbonated water.

❑ I try to average 9 hours of sleep a night. While I can get by on less, that's exactly the problem: I don't like to "get by." Sleep is my recovery from living a full day. I used to have problems getting good sleep while traveling until I realized that, when on the road, I had to import my bedtime rituals from home. I don't watch television, but when I first started traveling, I would lie in bed, surfing channels, glassy-eyed, unable to fall asleep. So if I couldn't sleep, I should just watch more television, right? No. What worked at home would work when not at home. At home, I read before bed to calm my mind; now I do that in hotel rooms, too. And it works every time. In fact, I have trained myself so well that I can take a book on an airplane and be sound asleep before take-off. Sleep is recovery, and I will take all the recovery I can get.

Emotional:

❑ My daughter is my number-one priority and I find ways to be present with her though I may not physically be with her. When traveling, I call her every night before bed, we have regular webcam chats, I mail her cards and she has recordings of me reading her favorite books.

❑ My exercise routine is better than any drug. Running is my time to think about nothing or everything, depending on the day. It's my chance to hit my reset button. After an exercise session, I feel like myself again— no longer tense, stressed out, impatient or distracted. Instead, I'm focused, calm and energized. If I go more than three days without exercise, I become incredibly edgy. After 15 to 20 minutes of breathing hard and focusing on my body, my system returns to a state of balance.

Mental:

❑ I am the ultimate list maker. My life moves along at a good clip, and to stay on top of things and have a sense of control, I write everything down. It's on paper and out of my head, so there is room up there for other important things.

❑ I spend as much time as I can in the present moment. Human beings have such a sophisticated capacity to transport themselves through time that often they live most of their waking lives in the non-existent future—worrying about things that haven't happened—as well as the unchangeable past—regretting decisions or actions. Though I prepare for and anticipate future events, and always want to learn from my past experiences (especially my mistakes), I focus on the *now. "In what ways do I need to be extraordinary right now? Who or what should be receiving my full and best energy right now? What can wait?"*

Spiritual:

❑ Our spiritual energy ties in to our values and beliefs. Earlier, I said that I value using the skills I possess— and not just using them but applying them to their *full potential.* I make a point to get outside my comfort zone every day—whether it's attempting to understand a point of view or trying to beat my previous race time. I want to fully experience all the highs life has to offer, and even some of the lows. The lows? Yes. I learned by going through a very painful divorce that I can get through anything. While navigating my way through this especially difficult time, I realized that I—that pretty much all human beings—tend to avoid uncomfortable situations, no matter the ultimate cost. We live in a society where things come pretty easily to many of us; if it takes really hard work to get something, we may question how much we really want it. I have learned to embrace struggle, to accept pain. Although it may honestly feel like it, it's not going to kill me. I will learn from it, and be stronger for it.

❏ I want to be a prime example to my daughter, Isabella, that there are no limits in life. That if we work hard, even through times of discomfort, we can become anything. While I would prefer it if she didn't experience all the self-doubt that plagued me, I know at least some of that will be a part of her life, as with anyone's. My desire for her is that she grows into a strong, confident, caring individual with sound morals and a good sense of humor.

So, then: What's your definition of an athlete? Is it someone with the best equipment? The right clothes? To be an athlete, is it required that one must be coordinated?

Or is an athlete someone who gleans every last bit out of the full range of skills he or she possesses? Who "competes" at life by maximizing all his or her energy—not just physical but emotional, mental and spiritual? Who doesn't give up and aims at all times to find ways to exceed today's mark?

At 35, I'm in the best shape of my life. I'm the leanest I have ever been, the strongest, the fastest, the most flexible. I sleep great at night. I have tremendous energy despite a brutal travel schedule.

I am also the most competitive I have ever been. Not with other people but with myself. I want to know what I'm made of. While I live in the present, I can't wait to see what next year brings—how much stronger I will be. I can't wait to see my progression over the next five years—how much faster I will have become. Will I ever be an elite athlete? I highly doubt it. Will I have expanded my capacity? Absolutely. Will I continue to have great energy? No doubt about it. Will I push myself as hard in my career? Definitely. Will I continue to aspire to be the most amazing mother to my daughter? I think that one is obvious.

After all, her mother is an athlete.

Chapter 9

Religious Leader:
The Ultimate Corporate Athlete

by Jim Mellado

I first encountered the principles that comprise the corporate athlete solution in 2005 when we invited Dr. Jack Groppel to speak at The Leadership Summit, a conference experience offered every August designed to inspire and equip religious leaders to further the cause of Christ in their local church. More than 60,000 leaders attended from around the world, our biggest turnout to date. Jack's talk represented a radical moment: In the ten years of hosting Leadership Summits, we had never had a speaker address the role that physical fitness plays in determining a leader's engagement. For the first time, I saw an amazingly powerful, direct connection between a leader's level of physical fitness and his performance in ministry life. Incredible and even counterintuitive as it may sound, *the physical part of life is the God-given foundation for living fully engaged in all those dimensions we more naturally associate with our mission—the emotional part of life, the mental part and the spiritual part.*

Before that day, I understood that an athlete needed to be in shape to compete, but why, if I was spending all day sitting at a desk or in meetings, would *I* need to be particularly fit? It's not as if someone was timing me to see how fast I could get from one meeting to the next! Yet, in that Summit session, Jack drew a line from physical fitness, on one hand, to emotional, mental, and spiritual engagement and vitality, on the other. He made the case that if you neglect to care for your body, it will fail in *all* areas. It's just a matter of time.

It has been three years since Jack spoke. People who were fortunate enough to be at that transformative event still talk about changes they made in their lives from that day on. One pastor told me simply, "That session saved my life."

At the time, I felt I was in decent shape, but I didn't have the right perspective on staying fit as a leader; I lacked a strong "why" about my physical fitness. My "why" had more to do with my history of being an athlete. I didn't see the connection between full engagement at work and my fitness routines. In fact, I felt they were at odds with each other in competing for that precious commodity: my time. How could I possibly stop progress at work to go home and "play" (which is how I categorized the time I spent working out)? You didn't sacrifice work for play! Certainly not God's work! As for nutrition, I was 40 before I paid any attention to it. I had no idea how little I knew about the connection between diet and full engagement at work. I ate whatever I wanted, in the amount I wanted, when my schedule dictated. But in that plenary session, something shifted in my heart and mind. Investing in my body wasn't "play" anymore; it wasn't merely a "nice" thing to do, if you could. It would become an integral part of fulfilling my calling. Two years later, it would literally save my life.

While swimming at a beach in Baja California, my 13-year-old son and I were caught in a riptide. By the time Davy and I reached each other, we were so far out that I thought we weren't going to make it. In that moment, I resolved to give my son every ounce of energy I possessed to get him as close to shore as possible, in the hope that he could be saved. Being a former Olympic decathlete, I knew about pushing my body to the limit. I had done it many times before—or so I thought. What happened to me in the ocean, to get my son closer to shore, shattered that limit. Because of my extreme physical depletion and muscle breakdown, my body produced too much myoglobin in my blood, leading to complete kidney failure. The doctors told me that had I not been in the physical condition I was in, I would not have made it...nor would have my son. Furthermore, a year before this incident, Davy, on his own, began to invest in his physical condition and eating habits. His improved physical condition level helped save us both. I had enough energy to push a "contributor" who was swimming; I would not have had enough energy to pull a "victim" who needed rescuing.

I appreciate that most of those reading this won't ever find themselves in a similar life-and-death situation, a struggle that demands that level of physical conditioning to survive. However, should you dismiss my experience as one to which you can't relate, remember: *All our days are numbered.* In my case, a near-death experience made this fact more vivid than ever, but it was always true, and will always be true…and it's just as true for you right now. God used our fitness level to grant my son and I more days to continue His bidding on this Earth. He can do the same for you. Too many people, religious leaders among them, are reducing the number of their days by not taking care of themselves.

Your life as a leader influences others, perhaps more than you know. So paying attention to and taking care of your body is not just about you: It impacts those around you. A couple months after the swimming incident, I overheard my son Davy telling my wife that he started working out because he saw me doing it. My lifestyle influenced my son, who changed his lifestyle, which in turn helped save us both.

Not only will investing in your fitness and health likely increase the number of your days, but it will improve the quality of those days, too. Steve Aldana, an expert in healthcare, addresses this in his book, *The Culprit & The Cure*:

> "Individuals who eat right and exercise throughout their lives live longer. They still experience significant medical events toward the end of their lives, but on average, the events are delayed between 7 and 13 years, and the time between the significant medical event and death is shortened…It's as if living a healthy lifestyle allows you to live a full, rich life well into old age, at which time you become ill, experience a rapid decline in health and pass away."[1]

What happens when a good person dies prematurely because he or she didn't take care of the body? All the positive energy they produced that might have, *would* have, been used to do good works in the future gets shut off, permanently.

An act of kindness that might well have turned around someone's life is never committed.

An inspirational word goes permanently unspoken and, worse, unheard.

A chair is left empty at family gatherings.

There is one less person of substance to make the world a better place.

Tragic? Undoubtedly. Family and other loved ones lose out immeasurably. But when such a development happens to a religious leader, it also means this: A ministry to serve those in need simply is not created. A congregation does not become mobilized to help others. A vision for a better future is never conceived and, fair to say, we are worse for it. If the world were overloaded with love-driven leaders, perhaps losing a few here or there would, in the grand scheme, feel somehow acceptable. But we enjoy no such overflow, at least not now. So to lose even one of them for reasons we can control—reasons having to do with the care and stewardship of our own bodies—is beyond lamentable. It's tragic.

I have been frank about what does happen when a leader's life is abbreviated because the physical self was neglected; the dramatic absence of goodness is obvious. Less obvious are the consequences an impoverished physical condition has on a leader's energy level and performance.

Here are some real scenarios in the day-to-day life of the religious leader who fails to maintain and honor the physical self, and the consequences of such neglect:

1. He exhausts his energy 15 minutes before the end of a meeting, sabotaging the chance to get to the breakthrough idea that could transform the congregation.
2. She lacks patience with a non-performing employee, leading to a badly handled dismissal, which in turn leads to broken community and diminished respect for the leader.
3. He succumbs to sin in a vulnerable moment because his capacity to handle stress is significantly compromised.

4. She runs out of energy at the end of the workday, which leads to skimming to perfunctory interaction at home with the most important people in her life.

To young leaders, the topic of energy management may sound unnecessary. Physical energy is plentiful and easily renewable, right? Even for them, though, and more explicitly for older leaders, physical energy is a *finite* resource, which runs dry sooner than later without a strategy for full engagement.

I find it interesting—ironic perhaps, even hypocritical—that many of us in the religious subculture profess one set of beliefs on the issue of good health and fitness (that they are conditions to which one should aspire; that they are way up on the "food chain" of values because, absent of them, little else is possible), yet we proceed to behave in ways that aggressively contradict this belief. The body is the "temple of the Holy Spirit," we regularly remind congregants, in part to discourage abuses to that temple such as smoking, drinking, drug use and other physically destructive behaviors. But what of the physical ramifications of poor nutrition? What happens to you as a result of eating fatty, fried, highly sweetened, chemically shot-up foods? What of bad or non-existent fitness? By pretending that good nutrition, regular exercise, and sufficient sleep and recovery are not equally important values to promote, when we all know in our hearts that they are, we have essentially swapped, if unmaliciously, strong teaching, guidance and Scripture for avoidance, silence and acquiescence. We are capable of so much more.

It's understandable, of course. Meal time, for example, is a time for sharing, for being together, for many good things to happen—regardless of what kinds of food are eaten, or how much; indeed, it is a time characterized by bounty (and far less so by discipline). The community feeling engendered at mealtime was a major New Testament church reality—and there were no specific instructions regarding nutrition; only to appreciate the blessing of being free while being careful not to abuse that freedom for the sake of others.

Another falsehood we perpetuate (again, unmaliciously): The religious leader misapplies the core value of servanthood—the standard for congregational leadership—when he or she believes and acts as if it's okay, more than okay, to neglect and even abuse one's own body with poor eating habits, non-existent exercise, and scattered focus and time management...as long as that neglect is the result of tending to activities that directly help to meet the needs of others. Well-meaning as that belief is, it leads prematurely and inevitably to the leader's ineffectiveness, and possibly his or her demise, thus shortchanging the leader's ability to serve for the long haul.

What I am encouraging here, then, is hardly selfishness, self-centeredness, vanity or pride. I am encouraging the religious leader to accept, among his or her many obligations, one more: the imperative to care better. To understand the fundamental need for care and to learn how best to care. Only in this way can a leader honor the physical gifts that God gave us. And, as I have suggested repeatedly, this is vital not just for us but for those around us. The lack of information, or outright misinformation, about the role physical fitness plays in our lives, leads to unfortunate consequences that are hard to see in the short-term, but which affect our capacity to live healthy, fully engaged lives.

Jack Groppel's session at the Leadership Summit could not have come at a more opportune time for me in my vocational leadership role. Increasingly, I was feeling the huge demands of leading a ministry, co-parenting a growing family and fueling that engagement with what seemed to be shrinking reservoirs of energy. Should it not have made sense to me that the fitness of my body significantly determined my success in performing and expanding my leadership? That it might be likened to how an athlete's fitness directly determines his or her success? And yet, as Jack pointed out, athletes spend 90 percent of their time training and 10 percent performing, while corporate executives are just about the opposite—10 percent of their time training, 90 percent performing. In truth, *leaders mostly train on the job* as they perform. In this regard, religious leaders are similar to corporate executives.

Over the last 14 years, in my role as President of the Willow Creek Association (WCA), an international training organization with over 12,000 member churches, I have attempted to be a student of religious leaders' needs so that, with training and resources, the WCA may serve them better. I have noticed that the WCA tends to attract a more entrepreneurial, risk-embracing, outreach-oriented leader on average; that a WCA church tends to be several times larger than average and offers more challenges. Thankfully, most WCA churches are growing—but that means that their leaders must deal with the complications associated with growth.

However, most senior pastors, it's fair to say, were not trained to be land and building developers, team builders, conflict management experts, fundraisers, organizational architects, visionaries or financial gurus. If one is to be successful at heading a growing congregation, though, then these are roles in which one must thrive—on top of being (of course) a pastor, teacher, counselor, mercy giver and theologian. How many professions reward your success by forcing you to undergo on-the-job training in skill areas never addressed in your vocational training requirements? Yet it's true in the church world, for many reasons, primarily because the rate of change in the demands on religious leaders outpaces the ability of many pastoral training and educational institutions to keep up with these changes. Some seminaries are adjusting to the new realities; many are not. What remains are leaders living in the growing gap between what they are physically able to do and what they are expected to do.

I have observed that the first casualty in dealing with these new, often overwhelming challenges is the leader's own physical condition. Pressed for time, driven to meet the changing needs of the congregation while trying to be everyone's pastor, the leader starts to eat the wrong foods, in the wrong quantities, at the wrong time. He or she believes there is no time for exercise, that he or she cannot or should not make time for it—and, if somehow exercise *is* worked in, then it's frequently the wrong exercise, at the wrong time, in an inefficient way. Over time, naturally, the body starts to fail, along with the leader's ability to grow along with his or her congregation. He or she is left behind, feeling helpless, feeling unable to measure up.

It doesn't have to be that way.

The first major benefit I enjoyed when I applied the principles of the corporate athlete advantage to my own life was an increase in emotional energy. How critical was that? Religious leadership is nothing if not incredibly draining emotionally. We are asked to lead with decisiveness and strength, to learn how to make tough calls...but, at the same time, to grow love, safety and community among those we lead. When a corporate executive fires an employee, the executive can count on probably never seeing the ex-employee again; when a religious leader fires an employee, the ex-employee may still choose to attend that church! In the corporate world, organizations freely target the "best" customer segments to serve, ignoring the rest; in church work, leaders are compelled by mission to engage *all* people—the great and not-so-great, those with whom one has an affinity and those one doesn't, those that make one crazy, even enemies. Does any institutional entity target *all* people of the world, offering to meet *all* their needs and commit to eternal existence together in community? Yet that's precisely the mission of the church! If ever a group of leaders needed huge reservoirs of emotional energy, it's those in the church...however, its leaders are often the first to abuse the very thing God gave us to maximize our emotional capacities: our bodies. Religious leaders need to be in great physical shape to deal with their unique stresses. When a religious leader fails, it's usually not triggered by a spiritual or mental problem but an emotional one. But few of us make the connection between diminished physical fitness and diminished emotional capacity.

The second benefit I realized was an improved ability to manage stress. God created within all of us a deep common desire to grow and improve; indeed, it's positively unnatural for someone to desire to worsen, to go backwards, to lose hope for a better future. But growth never comes without stress. Growth, by its very definition, requires us to experience and endure stress as we walk into the new and unknown. Not that most (or any) of us *like* stress: It doesn't feel good, so we label it as something bad, something to be avoided. The corporate athlete solution rejects this notion. It contends that the presence of stress in our lives isn't the problem; the problem is our utter incompetence at how to *recover* from stress. Recovery is the key to helping us get back into growth mode...so we can handle even more stress! Proper recovery helps us to expand our capacity to handle gracefully all the emotional complexities and other stresses met by religious leaders. And, oh, how we need that: After all, stress in our lives is not about to be eradicated.

Recovery helps us not only to handle the stress that comes with our position; it also helps to stop the natural flow of sin in our lives when under significant pressure. How? The combination of great stress plus incompetent recovery strategies leave us terribly vulnerable to sin. Unmanaged stress creates a powerful drive to escape the pressure...and sinful behaviors often seem the most reasonable outlet. We even tend to excuse our sin by telling ourselves we *deserve* relief—albeit sinful relief—because of all the good we do through our leadership! Viewed logically, we know this is a gross rationalization. But in our weakened state, we accept it as an inevitable response.

Now, too many of us—religious leaders, other leaders and everyone else—believe that the way to "solve" the dysfunctional trait brought about by stress is to avoid stress altogether. To craft an existence of easy living, one far removed from stress. Yet that means we have built a life free from growth. *You cannot be a great leader and avoid stress.* Jesus couldn't and neither can we. The very nature of leadership drives us to new and unknown places in life. That's how leadership works. Leaders were not meant to run away from stress. And if we do, we will invariably find artificial, often self-destructive ways to fill the void created by an unchallenging life.

Therefore, if too much stress coupled with poor recovery strategies leave us vulnerable to inappropriate escapism when the pressure becomes too strong; and if too little stress leaves us unchallenged, seeking artificial, destructive forms of excitement to address our boredom...where are we supposed to find balance? How can we find a way of being that does not compromise our effectiveness as leaders?

I believe that the single greatest benefit religious leaders will enjoy from learning and applying the principles of the corporate athlete advantage is this: the gaining of new reservoirs of energy to better handle the unique emotional and spiritual stresses that come with leadership in the congregation.

But there is another important benefit still. Beyond the positive emotional and spiritual impact, the corporate athlete advantage also expands a religious leader's *mental* capacities. The exercise, eating and sleeping habits of typical religious leaders leave them frequently compromised: They cannot maximize the impact of their leadership gift. Superior leadership is in large part about making quality decisions, and such decision-making simply can't happen, not consistently, when one's brain is tired. Your brain is like a muscle; it gets tired when overused or misused. Athletes wouldn't consider going into competition in a state of fatigue. They take great care to rest before a big competition, to ensure they arrive at the arena fresh, with all their physical faculties rested. Any other approach makes peak performance impossible.

Yet other leaders—corporate, church, what have you—often make critical decisions while their minds are not prepared to handle the complexity of key decisions. The result? Mediocre decisions and inferior performance.

What is required of someone to make great decisions? One key, certainly, is for the mind to be clear, fully engaged and cognizant of all the crucial elements that need to be considered in the evaluation process. That's extensive mental activity, which requires a lot of mental energy. But how many of us know how our brain is fueled? Nutritionists do but not many more. What you eat, when you eat and in what amounts all have a profound effect in determining whether your brain is fatigued or properly fueled to perform at peak level when making decisions critical to your ministry. Actually, it's somewhat terrifying to think how many poor decisions have been and continue to be made by leaders in "brain drain" mode, simply because they did not know how to keep their mind properly energized.

It's not only that we are unaware of how to fuel our brains to maintain peak mental performance: There is another major obstacle to focused thinking. Doesn't it seem as if all the technological advances of our time—marvelous as they are—have conspired to degrade our ability to engage in quality-focused thinking? How can great leadership happen without quality focus? Our wireless capabilities are amazing…however, e-mailing and texting have become destructive, unbridled sources of interruption, the enemy of great thinking. Today, it's easier than ever for one's thinking agenda to get interrupted by anyone, anywhere, at any time, often with trivial issues. The tragic result is that we are kept almost constantly from the kind of deep contemplation and complex processing on which breakthrough ideas are built. Technology capabilities inundate leaders with hundreds of non-prioritized issues sent to them throughout the day, keeping the leader from focusing on the two or three truly crucial, urgent issues out of the hundred he or she receives. Yet how rare has it become to be able to think deeply on just a few that really matter?

To protect our precious thinking space, the corporate athlete advantage encourages us to implement rituals and systems. In essence, it implores us to be creative about these day-to-day technological barriers to creativity, so that we may once again be, well, creative. For example, I have two e-mail accounts. My assistant manages the account I release to the public, while I manage the one I provide to only a few strategic people. I never check my public e-mail; my assistant filters what comes my way through that channel. It keeps me from allowing the world control my mental agenda. I also set my PDA to *not* distract me every time a text message or e-mail arrives. If you are leading the meeting, set ground rules about how the team will deal with the technology interruptions. We have all been in countless meetings where people's PDAs go off regularly and it can be terrible for results; the person whose PDA just vibrated is now wondering who sent it, what it said, and if it might be important enough to leave the meeting, or even stop the meeting. Others might wonder the same. The agenda has just changed; focus is now diverted. If it's the PDA of the person leading the meeting, then everyone's attention is interrupted while the leader deals with the distraction. In a 1-hour meeting with eight people, you could easily have 25 interruptions! The result of this new technological reality is that you have surrendered your team's focus to anyone and everyone outside of that group that doesn't know (or care) about the problems the team is aiming to solve.

Another one of the many rituals encouraged by the corporate athlete advantage: Rather than multitasking, fully engage your attention in just one task. Multitasking is an attempt (a somewhat ineffectual and rarely fulfilling one) to engage the mind on more than one thing at a time, which, according to research, is an impossibility. Sequential processing is possible, however, and is about engaging the mind on only one task, then moving on to another. Technology, as I have mentioned, encourages constant multitasking, and if we do so, we lose our ability to perform well and to enjoy the moment. If we are truthful, many of us consider multitasking a leadership skill, not something that hinders quality thinking and relationships...yet, truthfully, is there anything more disrupting to building a quality relationship with others than watching them check their smart phone every 5 minutes?

We have all heard of athletes being in *the zone*—that "place" where they simply can't be denied from achieving what they want.

In sports, the scoreboard—visible to all; a finely calibrated measurement—reflects how the performance is unfolding in real time, making it obvious that the athlete is thriving. In the corporate world, there is stock price or annual revenue to tell you you are doing well (or not). In ministry leadership, though, one's overall success is rarely something that can be observed and judged in real time. There is no scoreboard—or, if one exists, the results of success or failure won't be posted for months or years. A poorly made decision is seldom seen for what it is until much later, and by then its centrality to some failure may be lost, covered over by other actions and circumstances. But when poor decisions occur—visible or not, obvious or not—someone inevitably is affected, often many people. Which is why religious leaders must understand how and when their minds perform at peak efficiency. They must know how to detect the signs of mental fatigue and avoid making key decisions.

Within four months of returning from the two-and-a-half-day corporate athlete executive program, the three of us that comprise the WCA Leadership Team who attended had lost a combined 50+ pounds, experienced significantly increased energy and felt more engaged by life; felt more *in* life. The profound lessons we learned emerged at just the right time for each of us because we had been in the midst of some of the most complex challenges we had yet to confront in our ministries. To chart the new course for the ministry, we needed to be fully engaged.

How did we achieve change? We improved our meeting formats: We scheduled regular breaks during long meetings; we provided healthy, low-glycemic snacks as well as plenty of bottled water. We trained our staff in what we had learned. We had no choice: We saw the results of the program's principles on our lives and needed to share them with others. We continue the dialogue with Jack Groppel and the Human Performance Institute to discover other ways we can maximize the beneficial effect of the principles on religious leaders and their congregants.

You certainly need not wait for us. You can start now. By taking the time to understand the corporate athlete solution and educate yourself about your body and how energy works, you will be honoring God for the physical gifts given. You will be able to love, give, solve, influence, teach more and live a more adventuresome life, knowing that you do it all in community with those you love, for as long as possible.

You will be glad you took the journey. Even more, your loved ones and congregants will reap what you sowed.

Chapter 10

Navy SEAL Training and
Energy Management

by Rear Admiral Ray Smith, U.S. Navy (retired)

We had received our mission! Seven days after Saddam Hussein invaded Kuwait, six USAF C-5 and C-141 aircrafts landed in San Diego. Within hours, we departed for Saudi Arabia with 160 Navy SEALs, special boat sailors and various other Navy specialists. We landed at the Saudi Air Base in Dhahran 36 hours later and offloaded our force and all its equipment.

Events were moving very quickly in early August 1990. There was genuine concern that Saddam would invade Saudi Arabia and create an even greater threat to the world's oil supply. So I was not surprised to be met at Dhahran by an Army major who informed me I was to send a platoon of Navy SEALs to a location just south of the border dividing Kuwait and Saudi Arabia. We had been given the mission to train the Saudi Army General Staff in how to direct tactical air strikes from the ground—something SEALs are trained to do. Thus, seven days after our arrival in the Kingdom, a SEAL platoon and support personnel departed our small, isolated base en route to the Saudi General Staff's position south of the Kuwaiti border. Our platoon's deployment was the first by any U.S. combat unit and reported directly to General Schwarzkopf's staff and ultimately the White House. A month later these remarkable young men successfully completed the mission and were relieved by the Army Special Forces. Soon thereafter, we were assigned additional missions with full expectation that we had the fitness and training to carry them out.

Thus began a seven-month experience characterized by uncertainty, stress and exceedingly long days. But first, the matter of finding a place to live. With a bit of foresight, I had contacted a SEAL officer in Bahrain prior to my departure and directed him to travel to Saudi Arabia—a relatively short drive across the causeway connecting the two nations—and find our team a place to "set up camp." In true SEAL fashion, he located an abandoned American beach compound circa 1960. Just what we needed. With the help of U.S. Army logistics, we moved people and equipment to this compound on the shores of Half Moon Bay. We remained there until a few short weeks before combat operations began in January 1991.

Half Moon Bay looked great—cabanas, sand volleyball courts, beautiful beaches…One minor problem, however, was the heat. August and September of 1990 still remain ingrained in my mind. The heat and humidity were unlike anything I had ever experienced. But I was confident in the overall fitness of my men, so I directed that we begin to secure our small camp and commence training for our wartime missions. It didn't take long to realize we were in a work environment unlike any to which we had ever been exposed. Hydration became our first and highest priority—in fact, the first two weeks in Saudi Arabia were devoted almost solely to obtaining an adequate supply of bottled water. Without consistent hydration during summer in Saudi Arabia, we were in grave danger. Nonetheless, establishing our camp and commencing training for our missions were required. So, as "tough" Americans, we trudged on during those first few weeks.

I soon realized that even with an adequate water supply, my men were prone to severe dehydration, sometimes fainting, due to the heat, humidity and our inability to adapt to the climate. It soon became so serious that I ordered cots to be set up within the compound to supply immediate IV fluids containing electrolytes and glucose in the event someone lost consciousness. Added to the complexity of our work environment was our inability to provide our own food. Half Moon Bay had no dining facilities nor did we have the manpower to produce meals.

Later in August, it became apparent that I needed to review my team's capacity to balance our work environment and assigned tasks with our individual capacity—that is, our energy to carry out commands. As Dr. Jim Loehr and the Human Performance Institute have identified in world-class athletes, corporate leaders and many, many others, we were experiencing a human energy crisis.

Energy management became even more complicated when the 20-mile trip to Dhahran for our meals began to grow burdensome. The men began to look for workarounds—most of which consisted of "convenience store" food bought at the Air Force Exchange. I confess to often falling victim along with my men. But the heat with its inevitable dehydration and severe loss of critical electrolytes remained our most formidable challenge.

One strength of Navy SEALs is the repetitive training to adapt to high-risk operational skills such as parachuting and diving. For example, scuba diving training in the SEALs is markedly more stressful than recreational scuba training. The SEALs are purposely harassed and forced to solve their equipment problems (created by SEAL instructors) without surfacing. Since the natural reaction is to swim to the surface, doing so during an actual SEAL mission could prove fatal. Thus, SEALs develop rituals or habits which become non-conscious and enable the individual to confront high-stress situations by managing emotional energy. In the case of scuba training, they are trained to stop, relax and assess the situation. They also learn that rituals which do not support one's job can be catastrophic. This was the case for all of us in Saudi Arabia during the summer of 1990. We had naïvely attempted to replicate our daily American rituals and habits in a physical environment simply not supportive of such routines. Finally, after about three weeks, I realized that we had made a most serious error. We had failed to observe the habits and rituals of those who had lived in the desert for 2,000 years! The Saudis arose very early in the day and worked until nine o'clock in the morning. During the heat of the day, they relaxed and restored their energy. About 4 p.m. they returned to work and finished at 8 or 9 p.m. How novel!

So with some chagrin, we began the process of changing our daily schedule to one used by the Saudis. Rising between 3 and 4 a.m., our team traveled to Dhahran for a very early breakfast, returned to camp and worked until 9 a.m. Like the Saudis, we stopped work during the hottest part of the day, returning to work around 4 p.m. So we only had to change a habit most Americans have made a central part of their daily lives from childhood. Simple, right? A rather simple-appearing change to a deeply ingrained habit can be extremely difficult, even if the new habit affords obvious benefits. It ultimately worked but not without a significant investment of self-discipline by all involved. Once the change became a habit, however, it was not seen as a change but rather a non-conscious habit within which very little energy was expended.

There were those, however, who chose to disregard breakfast for the extra sleep. There were also those whose workload was so demanding that they felt it imperative to skip breakfast. I happened to fall into that category and was probably the worst violator! Commanding the SEALs during Desert Shield and Desert Storm was probably the most challenging and high-stress environment I had ever been confronted with. As I look back to my early experience in Desert Shield, I was required to make important decisions almost daily, some without all the necessary information and others without understanding the physical environment in which we would be operating.

In order to be fully engaged in one's work and, by extension, one's life, one needs to develop positive rituals to balance one's expenditure of energy with energy renewal. With this in mind, let's review my new daily schedule. You recall our day began at 3 or 4 a.m. but stopped at 9 a.m. due to the humidity and heat. During that period, the men drove 20 miles to and from our camp for breakfast. I chose to skip breakfast in order to read and answer the many operational messages which arrived during the night. I also found that the only time to run was just prior to dawn. So I developed my own schedule, which I believed enabled me to not only avoid wasting time driving to breakfast but also permitted me to run daily. So here is how my morning schedule worked:

4:00 a.m. - 5:30 a.m.	Awaken and process operational messages (plus two to three cups of coffee).
5:30 a.m. - 6:30 a.m.	Run 4 to 6 miles. Shower.
7:00 a.m.	Staff meeting and more coffee.

Unfortunately, my schedule was aligned with the belief that time management was the most important factor in carrying out my mission! Not surprisingly, I soon realized that I was not performing as a productive and positive member at my own morning staff meetings. Although I had proudly crafted a precise schedule through impeccable time management, I was not bringing the required energy to the table when necessary. Frankly, I was not fully engaged.

Let's discuss what I had done to myself for the cause of time management. First, we were in a habitual state of dehydration—not acute but always present. After waking, I would normally drink two to three cups of coffee that in some cases functions as a diuretic, thereby exacerbating my dehydrated state. At the same time, I disregarded the fact that blood sugar levels are at their lowest upon awakening. Running 6 miles prior to my staff meeting further lowered my blood sugar to a point bordering on hypoglycemia. But, let's not forget, I was managing time, not energy! Not surprisingly, very shortly after our arrival, I found that my 7 a.m. staff meetings were not going as well as I would have expected. At the time, I somehow hadn't pieced together the impact of dehydration, caffeine, low blood sugar and lack of sleep in a high-stress environment. I knew the impact of each singularly but not their combined effect on physical, mental and emotional energy. I soon realized I was proving to be a negative influence during the meetings. Since I also held a staff meeting at 8 p.m. in the evening, I decided to have my Chief of Staff conduct the morning staff meeting. I made that decision not because I understood fully the negative implications of "time management," but because I sensed I was imparting negative energy into an already high-stress environment. It was only many years later, while working with Jim Loehr and HPI, did I finally realize the problem I had put myself in by trying to manage time, not energy. Fortunately, I had a Chief of Staff who did not miss breakfast!

The bottom line in this story is that providing positive, creative and incisive leadership while dehydrated, hypoglycemic, sleep-deprived and "caffeinated" occurs only by exception, not as a rule.

Interestingly, my evening staff meetings (which I chaired) were upbeat, positive and productive. Why? Not surprisingly, during the day I managed to put balance into my system through food, water and no coffee. As my staff would say, "No idea was a bad idea at the evening staff meeting!" My staff quickly learned to floor new ideas in the evening, never in the morning.

The lesson is simple and applies to all of us. Regardless of our own personal energy capacity—physical, emotional, mental and spiritual—our lives present a constant series of challenges and stress. SEALs arguably go through the most challenging military training in the world. Despite this, as a group we were operating with an *old story*—that is, we were the most fit, aggressive and energetic unit in the military, so we had only to "gut it out" as we did during basic SEAL training. Only through reassessing our new "working environment" did we adapt our energy management to cope with the new demands of the working environment. The good news in this story is that the young Navy SEALs who represented our country in Desert Storm adapted to their environment and conducted over 200 successful combat operations without injury. Their record of achievement during Desert Storm was the equal of any military unit who participated in that campaign.

The story of the SEALs in Desert Storm is, in many ways, a metaphor for life in today's high-stress, oftentimes disconnected and ever-evolving work environment. Adapting to our dynamic world is the single, most daunting challenge each of us must confront as we balance our work, family and health. Those who volunteer to become Navy SEALs are a powerful example of balancing one's life in a high-stress environment. To be a successful SEAL, a young man must first reconcile within himself the reasons for his decision to challenge the most difficult of military careers. The performance coaches at HPI will tell you that each of us has to confront his or her story as it pertains to one's goals. For every man, success in basic SEAL training derives its source of energy not from the potential glamour or recognition of being a SEAL but from a deeply rooted spiritual commitment. The young men who ultimately succeed have clearly faced the truth in their lives and developed a "story" which reflects their real purpose. An interesting example of how refusing to face the truth results in failure to meet life goals occurs when a son of a Navy SEAL decides to follow in his father's footsteps. Almost without exception, the young man soon realizes that without the spiritual energy flowing from deeply held personal goals, the chance of completing the mission is marginal. It simply is too much to expect that a young man can stay fully engaged for six months without having faced the truth about one's purpose for going to SEAL training. Very often, highly educated, successful athletes with superb physical skills do not succeed because they lack the emotional and spiritual energy to call upon when physical and mental energy are not sufficient.

In the end, Navy SEALs, like most of us, strive to find the pathway from ordinary to extraordinary. In the case of those aspiring to become Navy SEALs, the pathway to success ultimately resides in energy management. Interestingly, the 25-week basic SEAL course is, to a great extent, based on time. Whether treading water, running, swimming, negotiating the obstacle course or a myriad of other challenges, the unit of measure is time. But like the vast majority of society, time is peripheral to real success in life. It is how one makes use of that time that enables one to negotiate the pathway from ordinary to extraordinary. Since a typical day in SEAL training lasts 12 to 14 hours, managing one's energy is extremely critical to success. If, for example, a timed 4-mile run is scheduled at 4 p.m., it would be imperative for the student to retain hydration and blood sugar throughout the day. Oftentimes, lunch is time constrained, thereby necessitating a basic understanding of what foods to eat—for example, recognizing the difference between high- and low-glycemic goods and the importance of hydration. A SEAL student can be a naturally gifted runner but still fail to run a successful time if he is hypoglycemic and/or dehydrated.

The young SEAL candidates will also grapple with the importance of mental and emotional energy throughout their careers but especially so in SEAL training. One of the first tests students are confronted with is called drown proofing, a pool event in which the student must tread water in a pool for several minutes with hands tied behind the back and feet tied. Physically, this is a very simple test, but mentally and emotionally it can be highly intimidating. This is an experience where the young man learns the difference between opportunity-based and survival-based emotional energy. Remaining calm and mentally focused enables the student to succeed to have opportunity-based energy. Ultimately, almost every young man successfully completes this test—especially when they realize that practically everyone before them has completed the test also. Tests such as these oftentimes appear to be based on physical energy or skill. On the contrary, however, they enable Navy SEALs to marshal the necessary mental and emotional energy during periods of extreme stress.

As a Navy SEAL for 31 years, I can say that the real "strength" of a SEAL lies in the ability to develop habits that optimize mental and emotional (opportunity-based) energy. Most of us can become physically fit and through proper diet, sleep, etc. control our physical energy. However, the key to full engagement for a SEAL is maintaining a high level of physical fitness supported by ritual-based mental and emotional energy. This, and a strong sense of purpose (spiritual energy) prepares SEALs to confront any mission with full confidence. The SEALs' record of achievement is clear evidence that the path from ordinary to extraordinary is based on investing in all four dimensions of energy.

But energy management for all Navy SEALs also demands sufficient attention be paid to rest and recovery. This cyclic aspect of energy management is nowhere more obvious than in SEAL training. The average age of a typical SEAL student—which I found to be consistent during my own tenure as Director of Basic Underwater Demolition/SEAL (BUD/S) Training—is 22. Despite this seeming advantage of youth, the intensity and duration of energy investment during a five-day training week demand a balance with great weekend rest. This includes not only physical but also mental and emotional rest. The level of stress in all energy dimensions during SEAL training and on actual SEAL operations depletes the stores of energy in even the most capable young man. The hours comprising a weekend are critical to navigating the pathway from ordinary to extraordinary in preparing each student for the next week's training. Corporate athletes should take heed of the SEALs' emphasis on energy recovery. Taking one's work home in the evenings and weekends prevents energy recovery and compromises energy stores needed to fully engage with family and friends, while also preparing for the next day's mission.

As corporate athletes move into positions of greater leadership, the demands, responsibilities and pressure continue to increase. Managing a division of 20 employees compared to a department of 100 employees is not a linear function. A corporate athlete unprepared for this change will, in most likelihood, be unable to fully engage at his or her new level. Navy SEALs have recognized this and challenge themselves both as individuals and as teams throughout their career. Prior to the war on terror, SEALs were familiar participants in all the world's top adventure races, pushing themselves beyond their limits even though there was no military requirement to do so. It was simply a case of a SEAL's recognition that events like adventure races place the individual in an environment where more than simple physical energy is required. Though running 10K races is great physical endurance training, it does little to challenge the mental, emotional and spiritual sources of energy. As one who has completed numerous marathons, 300-mile and 350-mile adventure races, I can state unequivocally that, as challenging as marathons are, they are a one-dimensional event. Unfortunately, all of us live in a multi-dimensional environment and cannot depend on "marathon" fitness alone to deal with our complex existence. Adventure racing combines extreme physical stress with sleep deprivation, nutritional needs and cognitive stress in the form of land navigation. Such events are made to order for Navy SEALs because they have been trained to marshal all four forms of energy in carrying out their assigned missions.

This philosophy, so effectively described and taught at the Human Performance Institute, is alive and well within the SEAL culture. It retains its validity and enormous value within the SEALs because it works. Just as corporate athletes must possess the capacity to make quick, coherent decisions throughout long workdays, so do Navy SEALs while conducting missions. SEALs cannot deposit energy while conducting missions—nor can corporate athletes.

A last word on positive rituals...In 1998, my final assignment in the Navy took me back to the Pentagon where I had served 15 years prior. During my first assignment in the Pentagon and for most of my career thereafter, I was able to choose the time of day to exercise (the exception being Desert Storm). However, my assignment as Admiral precluded me from taking an hour and a half in the middle of the day to exercise.

Faced with this "incursion" into my long, cherished and intense ritual of a flexible exercise schedule, I pondered my options. Evening workouts were out—evenings were to be devoted to my family. Also, it was too easy at the end of a long day to use fatigue as an excuse not to exercise. Thus, the only option was early morning exercise.

So I began the effort of establishing a new ritual—up at 4 a.m., to the fitness center at 5 a.m., workout complete at 6 a.m. and off to work at 7 a.m. As much as I cherish my physical fitness, establishing this ritual required focused discipline every day. Ultimately, I prevailed—although I had to essentially "fall out of bed" on Friday mornings!

Now, six years later, I still adhere to that ritual. In fact, it is now so established in my corporate athlete program that I actually look forward to getting up at 4 a.m. and starting my workout at 5 a.m. No one could have told me 20 years ago that I would be maintaining my fitness using such a routine.

HPI's focus on the importance of building positive habits and rituals as the key to energy management is the single most critical factor for all of us on our journey from ordinary to extraordinary. No one has ever said the journey would be easy. Mustering the discipline to establish positive habits is not a trivial task. It is, however, achievable.

As you contemplate your journey from ordinary to extraordinary, remember what the Navy SEALs say about "easy." I'm not sure how or when this proverbial catchphrase evolved, but it was well known and highly respected when I went through SEAL training in 1969. It reflects the realization that none of us goes through life without challenges and was meant to encourage the young men when everything seems to be collapsing around them during SEAL training. It goes like this: "The only easy day was yesterday."

Remember these words when you have rewritten your story and begun to build into your life the habits and rituals to use on your journey from ordinary to extraordinary. I guarantee you will look back on your experience and think of the young Navy SEALs up to their necks in the surf at two in the morning singing songs to the instructors— while they suffer the cold of the Pacific Ocean. One thing rings true and carries them forward..."The only easy day was yesterday!"

Chapter 11

Clean Renewable *Human* Energy

by Will Marre

When I first began working with the Human Performance Institute, I was struck between the eyes with the company's 30 years of research and work with top world number-one athletes, SWAT teams, Special Forces and, more recently, with executives of Procter & Gamble, PepsiCo and GlaxoSmithKline in creating nothing short of a corporate cultural revolution. A revolution that is sorely needed in an age of radical competitiveness.

You see, the *technology* revolution of the past 15 years has created a new global playing field, a change that is as stunning as the industrial revolution of 200 years ago. We find ourselves in a new economy characterized by two driving forces.

Driving force number one is a consumer demand for unique value. There is simply no way to keep margins high and sales increasing with yesterday's products. Organizations must create a *Unique Value Advantage* that is creatively packaged, communicated and delivered in a seamless brand system, or their products will be increasingly ignored. And that's a problem. We have a vast oversupply of nearly every imaginable product or service. All you have to do is visit any supermarket or retail website to know that the world is flooded with competitors, most of them trying to be different in the same way. Very little is unique. Or original.

This brings us to *driving force number two* and the focus of the remainder of this chapter: employees' demand to work in environments that promote creativity and honor talent. Workers no longer respect empty bureaucracies and mind-numbing hierarchies. Today's talent is attracted to organizations that are institutions for new ideas and brilliant execution. The war for talent isn't just to hire the best; it's to ensure your best people thrive.

It's these driving forces that make HPI's work so suitable for our time. For decades they have helped athletes and experts in high-stress professions beat their competitors by creating innovative solutions, on the spot, in real time.

Dr. Jim Loehr, Chairman, CEO and Co-Founder of the Human Performance Institute, is a performance psychologist. Years ago he noticed that when professional tennis players fell behind in key matches, they often began to construct a story of why they lost before the match was over. Between points their minds were flooded with an imagined post-match press conference where they conjured up canned excuses for poor performance (blisters, ankle sprains, bad officiating). Jim learned that champions, however, never "lose" before the match is over. They keep their focus on the game, looking for an edge, *any* edge. They are willing to try new, potentially winning strategies and abandon losing ones. They are willing to change their pace, their rhythm. They improvise and try new approaches to upset their competitors or set new standards of play. What Jim realized is that this unyielding, innovative mindset relies on high mental energy possible only when the player has high reserves of physical stamina, emotional balance and mental focus. This doesn't happen without training. It also doesn't happen without tapping into the biological oscillation of energy that enables the player's brain to be optimal at creative problem-solving and improvising in the midst of competition.

Here is the challenge.

The *value* work generates has evolved over the past decades. *Process* work such as manufacturing and *knowledge* work such as accounting are increasingly going to a low-cost worldwide workforce. Most of this is skilled work that is routine and highly structured. For this type of work, time and reliability are valued. But this form of labor is now becoming a commodity. Virtually any business can access thousands of skilled routine workers. What we used to call productivity does not equate to value in today's marketplace. Increasingly, value comes from creativity, innovation and invention. This requires something greater than workers' *time*. It requires what Jim Loehr calls *Full Engagement*. And full engagement requires drawing on four dimensions of energy: physical, emotional, mental and spiritual.

Evolution of Work Value

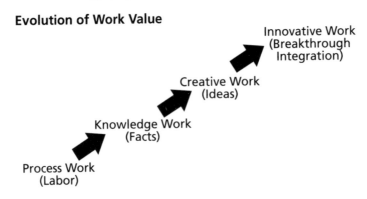

Figure 3

To create business cultures of high engagement requires a new mindset of leadership. This is the mindset of *Unique Value Creation*: solving problems that were previously unsolvable; inventing products that delight us beyond our ability to imagine them before they appear. Like training tennis players to not give up, we must develop employees who will be light on their feet, nimble, creative, able to think on the fly and who will not give up. And leaders must be able to build teams that respond to disruptive competitive threats as they arise, or even better, *become* the disruptive competitive threat to others.

The Human Performance Institute and their clients are discovering that human creativity requires high amounts of human energy. This isn't just a hyperbole; it's a biological, emotional and mental certainty. It works like this. Human physical energy—characterized by alertness and stamina—requires blood sugar levels and oxygen uptake that optimize both our metabolism as well as our brain chemistry. In other words, our creative brains require a steady diet of healthy foods and frequent exercise. The diet and daily lifestyle of most managers and leaders are not conductive to high levels of creative thinking and complex problem-solving. Too often we skip breakfast for coffee and a bagel, which is not a real breakfast. We tend to spike our blood glucose levels by eating simple sugars and carbohydrates to get us through an extended meeting and pull us out of afternoon drowsiness. But our poor eating habits drive our blood sugar so high we are flooded with insulin and fall into an energy deficit. These quick fixes turn out not to be fixes at all. Instead, our fluctuating blood-sugar levels drive our brains, our attention and our moods outside of our sustainable high-performance zone, leaving us in a perpetual "hangover" of fatigue.

This, combined with sleep deprivation and stimulus overload from a flood of unedited information, makes us poorer problem solvers, collaborators and entrepreneurial thinkers than we are otherwise capable of being. The resulting stress stimulates a brigade of hormones that reduce judgment while increasing impatience and irritability. We end up with high-friction business cultures where our employees become less able to add value. Going without good food, exercise or sleep always produces the same result: sub-optimal human performance.

And it isn't just our poor eating habits that are making us less creative; we have a similar problem with *distraction* caused by trivial over-communication. E-mails and cell phones are great servants but poor masters. Studies show that the more senior leaders engage in day-to-day e-mail threads or, worse, compulsively read e-mails as they come in, the less time they give to strategic thinking. This is a classic case of becoming lost in the clutter while big decisions involving foresight, creativity and judgment are tragically missed.

In fact, the first "commandment" of top performing athletes is "Thou shalt focus." Focus on the point, the shot, the task at hand. One often hears athletes in post-game interviews talking about the need to control distractions. They know distractions kill performance. But focus is not only critical to athletic performance; it is also essential to both creativity and strategy execution. Can we imagine Michelangelo chipping away on his David sculpture while talking on a cell phone or climbing down the scaffolding of the Sistine Chapel to check his latest e-mail alert? Yet research confirms that in most modern work environments, places starved for fresh ideas and clear thinking, we are suffering from chronic attention deficits.

Published in the *Harvard Business Review*, research reveals that the constant onslaught of unprioritized information results in impulsive decisions, anger, frustration and persistent feelings of overwhelm.[1] Other research estimates on lost productivity from interruptions are close to US$588 billion annually.[2] Why so much? It turns out that employees devote an average of 11 minutes to a project before they are interrupted. Like carbohydrate-loading hummingbirds, we flit from one task to the next, achieving little of value or depth in any one pursuit. In many tests pitting multitaskers against single-focused workers, the multitaskers are significantly slower and more error prone. Through brain research using magnetic imaging, we now know why multitasking workplaces under-perform and exhaust their employees. It seems that bouncing from one task to the next in an endless cycle stimulates visual centers of the brain and produces dopamine, giving multitaskers a false high. We think we are being productive when we are not. In the meantime the higher brain centers related to judgment, memory and learning are turned off. If multitasking persists, stress hormones such as cortisol begin to flood our entire bodies, causing anxiety and fatigue.[3]

So what does all this mean for leaders who are trying to stimulate creativity, innovation and strategic focus? Plenty. Today's business-as-usual work cultures are making us less able to do the very things employees need to do to produce unique value. Employees need structured, uninterrupted creative time, regular periods of large muscle movement (like walking or climbing stairs) and even daily "corporate recess" to connect with colleagues in a relaxed atmosphere. What HPI has learned from over 30 years of helping athletes and corporate high performers succeed is that we cannot ignore our own design. Our biology, brain chemistry and oxygen uptake systems directly impact our ability to perform and especially to *excel* at the higher challenges of creativity, collaboration and judgment needed in today's hyper-competitive world.

Clients like Procter & Gamble are acutely aware of the edge that unique innovation gives to their US$68 billion business. With over 300 brands and more than 160 companies, it could be argued that P&G's primary business process is innovation. What is required to sustain creative and collaborative engagement is a daily rhythm that creates time for reflection, communication and exercise. Only then is human energy optimized toward its highest levels of contributions.

P&G is constantly seeking to create organizing frameworks that serve creativity and stimulate passion and initiative from their people. Not only does this mean getting employees to be at their mental, emotional and physical best, it also includes a spiritual component of uniting people around a mission that matters. Procter & Gamble is deeply committed to eliminating internal cultural practices that waste talent. It is willing to over-invest in practices that set a new standard. For instance, their Connect + Develop research and development program has attracted over 90,000 scientist partners into a global innovation network that connects the talents and technologies of P&G's best minds with innovators and scientists around the world. It is a model of energetic collaboration.

In 2007, A.G. Lafley, CEO of Procter & Gamble, decided to make a high human energy culture a distinct competitive advantage. He enlisted the help of the Human Performance Institute to certify and train over 200 internal coaches to teach their employees principles of sound nutrition, restful sleep, productive meetings, task focus and daily rituals of renewal. This has helped employees to be physically energized, emotionally connected, mentally focused and spiritually aligned. In an age where less than 30 percent of Americans are fully engaged in their work,[4] this indeed is a departure from the norm.

What the world is thirsting for is clean renewable energy. Not just for industry, our homes or cars, but for ourselves. It's irresponsible to waste fuel and create green house gases. For instance, 85 percent of the potential energy in a gallon of gasoline is currently being wasted. That doesn't sound too different from how many organizations waste the creative energy of their own people. The Human Performance Institute has developed an executive program called the *Corporate Athlete* that optimizes the core sources of human energy. It ritualizes structured behavioral routines that promote high mental, emotional and physical functioning. Together these tools create a new, expanded reservoir of human energy for the organization as it faces its competition.

A few years ago, HPI's coaches began joking with audiences, "What if you had a boss that asked you when you arrived at work if you had a good breakfast, slept enough and if you had scheduled exercise for today? And then really rewarded you when you did?" But what started as a joke is increasingly becoming part of organizational strategy for client organizations developing cultures designed to thrive in this new revolutionary global economy. In the end, it's rather simple. What optimizes the individual human talent of an organization will also optimize the whole organization's sustained long-term results. Managing energy is a paradigm shift that offers an extraordinary competitive edge in the world of business today. This is an idea whose time has come.

References

Introduction

1. Centers for Disease Control and Prevention. (2008). *Overweight and Obesity: Introduction*. Retrieved September 9, 2008, from http://www.cdc.gov/nccdphp/dnpa/obesity.

2. Isidore, C. (2005, January 28). *P&G to Buy Gillette for $57B*. Retrieved September 9, 2008, from http://www.money.cnn.com/2005/01/28/news/fortune500/pg_gillette.

3. Murphy, C. (2006, July 10). The CEO Workout. *Fortune, 154*(1), 43-44.

4. O'Kelly, E. (2006). *Chasing Daylight*. New York: McGraw-Hill.

5. Murphy, C. (2006, March 20). Secrets of Greatness: How I Work. A.G. Lafley. *Fortune, 153*(5), 74-76.

Chapter 1

1. Powers, S. and Howley, E. (2003). *Exercise Physiology: Theory and Application to Fitness and Performance*. (5th ed.). New York: McGraw-Hill.

2. Lloyd, D. and Rossi, E. (1992). *High Frequency Biological Rhythms: Functions of Ultradians*. New York: Springer-Verlag.

3. Kellmann, M. and Kallus, K. (1999). Mood, Recovery-Stress State and Regeneration. In: Lehmann, M., Foster, C., Gastmann, U., Keizer, H. and Steinacker, J., editors. *Overload, Fatigue, Performance Incompetence and Regeneration in Sport*. New York: Springer. pp. 101-117.

4. Kemp, P. (2004, October). Presenteeism: At Work—But Out of It. *Harvard Business Review*, 49-58.

5.   Lien, M., Ruthruff, E. and Johnston, J. (2006). Attentional Limitations in Doing Two Tasks at Once. *Association for Psychological Science, 15(2)*.

6.   Rossi, E.L. (1991). *The 20 Minute Break: Reduce Stress, Maximize Performance, Improve Health and Emotional Well-Being Using the New Science of Ultradian Rhythms*. Los Angeles: J.P. Tarcher.

7.   Williams, J., Trinklein, F. and Metcalfe, C. (1994). *Modern Physics*. New York: Holt, Rinehart and Winston, Inc.

8.   Bargh, J. and Chartrand, T. (1999). The Unbearable Automaticity of Being. *American Psychologist, 54,* 462-479.

9.   Pascual-Leone, A. et al. (1995). Modulation of Muscle Responses Evoked by Transcranial Magnetic Stimulation During the Acquisition of New Fine Motor Skills. *Journal of Neurophysiology, 74(3)*: 1037-1045.

10. Lutz, A., Brefezynski-Lewis, J. and Davidson, R. (2004). *Loving, Kindness and Compassion Meditation Results in Unique Patterns of fMRI Activation and Enhances the Reactivity of the Insula/Cingulate Neural Circuitry to Negative Stimuli in Meditators*. Slide presentation at the Society for Neuroscience.

11. Begley, S. (2007). *Train Your Mind, Change Your Brain: How a New Science Reveals Our Extraordinary Potential to Transform Ourselves*. New York: Ballantine Books.

Chapter 3

1.   McArdle, W.D., Katch, F.I. and Katch, V.L. (1994). *Essentials of Exercise Physiology*. Malvern: Lea & Febiger.

2.   Bouchard, C., Shephard, R. J. and Stephens, T. (1992). *Physical Activity, Fitness and Health: International Proceedings and Consensus Statement*. Champaign: Human Kinetics.

3.   Wilmore, J. and Costill, D.L. (1994). *Physiology of Sport and Exercise*. Champaign: Human Kinetics.

4.   Brooks, G.A. and Fahey, T.D. (1984). *Exercise Physiology: Human Bioenergetics and Its Applications*. New York: John Wiley & Sons.

5.   Balady, G. J. et al. (2000). *American College of Sports Medicine. ACSM's Guidelines for Exercise Testing and Prescription*. (6th ed.). Philadelphia: Lippincott, Williams & Wilkins.

6.   Haskell, W.L. et al. (2007). Physical Activity and Public Health: Updated Recommendation for Adults from the American College of Sports Medicine and the American Heart Association. *Medicine & Science in Sports & Exercise, 39*(8), 1423-1434.

7.   National Institute of Health (NIH) & National Institute of Neurological Disorders and Stroke (NINDS). (2007). *Brain Basics: Understanding Sleep*. Retrieved September 9, 2008, from http://www.ninds.nih.gov/disorders/brain_basics/understanding_sleep.html.

8.   Kent, M. (1998). *The Oxford Dictionary of Sports Science and Medicine*. (2nd ed.). New York: Oxford University Press.

9.   National Institute of Mental Health (NIMH). (2002). *"Power Nap" Prevents Burnout; Morning Sleep Perfects a Skill*. Retrieved September 9, 2008, from http://www.nimh.nih.gov/science-news/2002/power-nap-prevents-burnout-morning-sleep-perfects-a-skill.shtml.

Chapter 4

1.   Hardy, G. (2004, April). The Burden of Chronic Disease: The Future Is Prevention. *Preventing Chronic Disease, 1*(2). Retrieved September 9, 2008, from http://www.cdc.gov/pcd/issues/2004/apr/04_0006.htm.

2.   Bondi, M.A., Harris, J., Atkins, D. et al. (2006). Employer Coverage of Clinical Preventive Services in the United States (From Evidence-Based Practice to Practice-Based Evidence). *American Journal of Health Promotion, 20*(3), 214-222.

3.   Lee, D. (1997). Employee Stress: The True Cost. *The John Liner Review, 11*(3), 33-38.

4.   Reichheld, F. and Sasser, W. (1990). Zero Defections: Quality Comes to Services. *Harvard Business Review, 68*(5), 105-111.

5.   Langdon, J. (2001, September). Americans Are Working Too Hard: Oxford Health Plans Survey. *USA Today*. Retrieved September

9, 2008, from http://www.findarticles.com/p/articles/mi_m1272/is_2676_130/ai_78256868.

6. Braun Consulting News. (2004-2005, Winter). *The Shrinking American Vacation: Stress, Absenteeism and Overtime, 7*(6). Retrieved   September 9, 2008, from http://www.braunconsulting.com/bcg/newsletters/winter2004/winter20044.html.

7. Harkins, P. (1998, October). Why Employees Stay: Or Go. *Workforce*, 74-78.

8. Yaffe, K. (2001, May 9). *Exercise Protects Against Cognitive Decline*. Presented at the annual meeting of the American Academy of Neurology and reported at http://www.findarticles.com/p/articles/mi_m0CYD/is_16_36/ai_78050837.

9. Douglas, M. *Penny-Wise and Pound-Foolish? How Wellness Will Separate Corporate Winners from Losers.* Retrieved September 9, 2008, from http://www.content.monster.ca/12824_en-CA_pl.asp.

10. Goetzel, R., Guindon, A., Turshen, J. and Ozminkowski, R. (2001). Health and Productivity Management: Establishing Key Performance Measures, Benchmarks and Best Practices. *Journal of Occupational and Environmental Medicine, 43*(1), 10-17.

11. Bertera, R. (1990). The Effects of Workplace Health Promotion on Absenteeism and Employment Costs in a Large Industrial Population. *American Journal of Public Health, 80*(9), 1101-1105.

12. Golaszewski, T., Snow, D., Lynch, W., Yen, L. and Solomita, D. (1992). A Benefit-to-Cost Analysis of a Worksite Health Promotion Program. *Journal of Occupational Medicine, 34*(12), 1164-1172.

13. Thompson, D. (1990, March). Wellness Works for Small Employers Too. *Personnel,* 26-28.

14. Sunoo, B. (1997). Wellness Pays Off. *Workforce, 76*(12), 52.

15. Chapman, L. (1996). *Proof Positive: Analysis of the Cost-Effectiveness of Wellness.* (3rd ed.). Seattle: Summex Corporation, 1996.

16. U.S. Corporate Wellness. (2008, February 8). *ROI-Based Analysis of Employee Wellness Programs.* Retrieved September 9, 2008,

from http://www.uscorporatewellness.com/USCW%20-%20White %20Paper%20(ROI%20Analysis).pdf.

17. Sjoberg, H. (1983). Physical Fitness and Mental Performance During and After Work. *Ergonomics, 23,* 977-987.

18. Gajendran, R. and Harrison, D. (2007). The Good, the Bad and the Unknown About Telecommuting: Meta-Analysis of Psychological Mediators and Individual Consequences. *Journal of Applied Psychology, 92*(6), 1524-1541.

19. Skarnulis, L. (2005, July 26). *Is Your Job Making You Fat?* Retrieved September 9, 2008, from http://www.webmd.com/diet/ features/is-your-job-making-you-fat.

20. Jones, F., O'Connor, D., Conner, M., McMillan, B. and Ferguson, E. (2007). Impact of Daily Mood, Work Hours and Iso-Strain Variables on Self-Reported Health Behaviors. *Journal of Applied Psychology, 92*(6), 1731-1740.

21. Prevent Disease. (1991) *Why Should Your Company Offer Worksite Wellness Programs? The Association for Fitness in Business.* Retrieved September 9, 2008, from http://www.preventdisease. com/worksite_wellness/worksite_wellness.html.

22. Corporate Wellbeing. (1991). *Scientific Research on How a Workplace Gym Will Reduce Absenteeism, Stress and Staff Turnover.* Retrieved September 9, 2008, from http://www.corporatewell being.co.uk/Docs/SCIENTIFIC%20RESEARCH%202005.pdf.

23. Shepherd, R.J. (1986). *Economic Benefits of Enhanced Fitness.* Champaign: Human Kinetics Publishers.

24. Pelletier, K. (2001). A Review and Analysis of the Clinical- and Cost-Effectiveness Studies of Comprehensive Health Promotion and Disease Management Programs at the Worksite. *American Journal of Health Promotion, 16*(2), 107-116.

25. Bailey, G. (1998). Training as a Recruitment Tool. *HR Focus, 75*(7), 11-12.

26. Marcus, M. (2000). Workouts at Work Can Sweeten Long Days, But Don't Cut Loose on the Boss. *U.S. News & World Report, 128*(24), 57.

27. Dutton, G. (1997). Nurturing Employees and the Bottom Line. *HR Focus, 74*(9), 1-4.

28. Smith, B. and Broslawsky, T. (2007, February). *Energy for Performance Power of Full Engagement: Level 3—Application of Skills Project Summary.* Raleigh: GlaxoSmithKline. See www. corporateathlete.com for more information.

29. Performance Programs, Inc. (2008, March). *A Follow-up Assessment of the Corporate Athlete Executive Course at the Human Performance Institute.* Old Saybrook. See www.corporateathlete. com for more information.

30. Anshel, M.H. and Kang, M. (2008). Effectiveness of Motivational Interviewing on Changes in Fitness, Blood Lipids and Exercise Adherence of Police Officers: An Outcome-Based Action Study. *Journal of Correctional Health Care, 14*(1), 48-62.

31. Anshel, M.H. and Kang, M. (2007). An Outcome-Based Action Study on Changes in Fitness, Blood Lipids and Exercise Adherence, Using the Disconnected Values (Intervention) Model. *Behavioral Medicine, 33*, 85-100.

32. Anshel, M.H. and Kang, M. (2007). Effect of an Intervention on Replacing Negative Habits with Positive Routines for Improving Full Engagement at Work: A Test of the Disconnected Values Model. *Consulting Psychology Journal: Practice and Research, 59*(2), 110-125.

Chapter 5

1. Rippe, J.M. (1999). *Lifestyle Medicine.* Malden: Blackwell Science.

2. Mellen, P.B., Gao, S.K., Vitolins, M.Z. and Goff, D.C., Jr. (2008). Deteriorating Dietary Habits Among Adults with Hypertension: DASH Dietary Accordance, NHANES 1988-1994 and 1999-2004. *Archives of Internal Medicine, 168*(3), 308-314.

3. Ogden, C.L., Carroll, M.D., Curtin, L.R., McDowell, M.A., Tabak, C.J. and Flegal, K.M. (2006). Prevalence of Overweight and Obesity in the United States, 1999-2004. *JAMA, 295*(13), 1549-55.

4. Catlin, A., Cowan, C., Heffler, S. and Washington, B. (2007). National Health Expenditure Accounts Team. National Health Spending in 2005: The Slowdown Continues. *Health Affiliation, 26*, 142-153.

5. Valentine, N., Darby, C. and Bonsel, G.J. (2008). Which Aspects of Non-Clinical Quality of Care Are Most Important? Results from WHO's General Population Surveys of "Health Systems Responsiveness" in 41 Countries. *Social Science & Medicine.*

6. Dorfman, L., Wallack, L. and Woodruff, K. (2005). More Than a Message: Framing Public Health Advocacy to Change Corporate Practices. *Health, Education and Behavior, 32*(3), 320-336.

7. Petersen, M.R. and Burnett, C.A. (2007). The Suicide Mortality of Working Physicians and Dentists. *Occupational Medicine, 58*(1), 25-29.

8. Aldana, S.G. (2001). Financial Impact of Health Promotion Programs: A Comprehensive Review of the Literature. *American Journal of Health Promotion, 15*(5), 96-320.

9. Lee, Y.Y. and Lin, J.L. (2008). Linking Patient's Trust in Physicians to Health Outcomes. *British Journal of Hospital Medicine, 69*(1), 42-46.

10. Anson, O., Antonovsky, A. and Sgy, S. (1990). Religiosity and Well-Being Among Retirees: A Question of Causality. *Behavior, Health and Aging, 1*, 85-97.

Chapter 6

1. National Safety Council. (2007). *Injury Facts, 2007 Edition.* Itasca: Author.

2. Public Law 259, 83rd Congress, 1st Session. (1953, August 13).

3. Kowalski, M. (1994). *A Missing Component in Your Emergency Management Plan: The Critical Incident Stress Factor.* U.S. Bureau of Mines. Retrieved September 9, 2008, from http://www.cdc.gov/niosh.

4. Toossi, M. (2005). Labor Force Projections to 2014: Retiring Boomers. *Monthly Labor Review, 128*(11), 25-44.

5. Bureau of Labor Statistics. (2007). *Non-Fatal Occupational Injuries and Illnesses Requiring Days Away from Work, 2006.* Press release USDL 07-1741. Washington: U.S. Department of Labor.

6. Chao, E. (2005, September 20). *World Congress on Safety and Health at Work.* OSHA Conference in Orlando. Washington: U.S. Department of Labor.

Chapter 7

1. Dychtwald, K. and Flower, J. (1988). *Age Wave: How the Most Important Trend of Our Time Will Change Your Future.* New York: J.P. Tarcher.

2. Dychtwald, K., Erickson, T.J. and Morison, R. (2006). *Workforce Crisis: How to Beat the Coming Shortage of Skills and Talent.* Boston: Harvard Business School Press.

3. Slater, R. (2002). *29 Leadership Secrets from Jack Welsh.* New York: McGraw-Hill Professional.

Chapter 9

1. Aldana, S.G. (2005). *The Culprit & the Cure: Why Lifestyle Is the Culprit Behind America's Poor Health and How Transforming That Lifestyle Can Be the Cure.* Mapleton: Maple Mountain Press.

Chapter 11

1. Hallowell, E.M. (2005, January 1). Overloaded Circuits: Why Smart People Underperform. *Harvard Business Review, 83*(1):54-62, 116.

2. Gaskin, J. (2008, January 8). Workplace Interruptions Cost $588B in Lost Productivity. *IT World.* Retrieved September 9, 2008, from http://www.smallbusiness.itworld.com/4939/lost-productivity-nlsnetworking-080108/page_1.html.

3. Raman, R. (2006, October 28). *The Dangers of Multi-Tasking.* Retrieved September 9, 2008, from http://www.sethigherstandards.com/dangers-of-multi-tasking.

4. Loehr, J. and Schwartz, T. (2003). *The Power of Full Engagement.* New York: The Free Press.

Biographies

Jim Loehr, Ed.D.

Dr. Jim Loehr, Chairman, CEO and Co-Founder of the Human Performance Institute, is a world-renowned performance psychologist, and author of 14 books including *The Power of Story* and co-author of the national bestseller *The Power of Full Engagement*. Jim appeared on The Oprah Winfrey Show where an entire program was devoted to his ground-breaking energy management training system and concepts. He has also appeared on *NBC's Today Show*, *ABC's Nightline with Ted Koppel*, *The CBS Evening News with Dan Rather* and *CBS Morning News* and his work has been chronicled in leading national publications including the *Harvard Business Review*, *Fortune*, *Newsweek*, *Time*, *U.S. News and World Report*, *Success*, *Fast Company* and *Omni*.

Jim has worked with hundreds of world-class performers from the arenas of sport, business, medicine and law enforcement including Fortune 100 executives, FBI Hostage Rescue Teams and Army Special Forces. His elite clients from the world of sport include: golfer Mark O'Meara; tennis players, Jim Courier, Monica Seles and Arantxa Sanchez Vicario; boxer Ray Mancini; hockey players Eric Lindros and Mike Richter; and Olympic gold medal speed skater Dan Jansen.

Jim possesses a Master's and Doctorate in Psychology, serves on several prestigious scientific boards and is a full member of the American Psychological Association, the American College of Sports Medicine, the National Strength and Conditioning Association, and the Association for the Advancement of Applied Sport Psychology.

Jack Groppel, Ph.D.

Dr. Jack Groppel, Vice Chairman and Co-Founder of the Human Performance Institute, is an internationally recognized authority and pioneer in the science of human performance, and an expert in fitness and nutrition. He is also an Adjunct Professor of Management at the J.L. Kellogg School of Management at Northwestern University.

Jack authored *The Corporate Athlete* book and developed the corporate athlete concept for his training program while serving as an Associate Professor of Kinesiology and Bioengineering at the University of Illinois helping both business executives and athletes increase performance levels. In 1992, he combined his program with Dr. Jim Loehr to form the Human Performance Institute, formerly known as LGE Performance Systems, Inc.

Jack was recently elected as a Vice President on the Board of Directors of the United States Professional Tennis Association. A Fellow in the American College of Sports Medicine, he is also a Board certified nutritionist in the American College of Nutrition and a former Research Associate to the U.S. Olympic Training Center. He served for 16 years as the Chairman of the National Sport Science Committee of the United States Tennis Association.

Chris Osorio

Chris Osorio serves as President of the Human Performance Institute overseeing company strategy, business development and strategic alliances.

Chris has more than 25 years of experience in business and a Master's degree in Organizational Development from Pepperdine University. He spent the first decade of his career in the investment banking business as a senior partner, general principal, author and speaker. In 1988, Chris joined the Covey Leadership Center, at the time a new emerging training and development business. He spent the next decade with the Covey Leadership Center as a senior consultant, presenter, and in a variety of leadership roles as Covey, now FranklinCovey, grew from US$3 million to over US$500 million in revenue.

Since joining HPI, Chris has provided strategic leadership, recruited key talent, and sparked a new era of significant growth in revenue and profits.

Raquel Malo, R.D.

As Senior Vice President of Executive Training and Director of Nutrition for the Human Performance Institute, Raquel Malo trains thousands of top corporate executives of Fortune 500 companies every year, and helped design and implement the Full Engagement Nutrition program component. She specializes in keynote speaking and group facilitation. Raquel possesses a Master of Science degree in Nutrition from Texas A&M University and a Bachelor of Science degree in Nutrition and Dietetics from the University of Florida. She is a Registered Dietitian and has specialized in Pediatric Nutrition.

Raquel has published and presented scientific findings from her nutrition research in a variety of professional publications. She frequently makes appearances on national radio and television as a nutrition expert. Her professional experiences include working as a community Clinical Dietitian in Dallas, Texas and as a Pediatric/Maternal Dietitian for the Department of the U.S. Army.

Raquel has also developed a national nutrition education and weight control program for online use. Besides, she is on the Blue Ribbon Advisory Board for PepsiCo, advising on health and wellness issues and strategies. Raquel's professional interests include nutritional genomics and disordered eating patterns.

Chris Jordan, M.S.

Chris Jordan is the Vice President of Facilitator Training for the Human Performance Institute, responsible for the Train-the-Trainer Program. As the Director of Fitness, he manages the development and execution of all corporate fitness programming. Chris holds a Master of Science degree in Exercise Physiology with distinction from Leeds Metropolitan University in the United Kingdom, and a Bachelor of Science in Applied Biological Sciences from the University of the West of England in Bristol, United Kingdom.

Prior to joining HPI, Chris was the Fitness Program Consultant for the U.S. Air Force in Europe, based at Royal Air Force Lakenheath base in the United Kingdom, and an exercise physiologist at the British Army Personnel Research Establishment of the Ministry of Defence. He has published research in the *Journal of Sports Sciences* and has written over 50 articles for U.S. Air Force publications, the *Army*

Health Connection newsletter, *Florida Tennis*, *Men's Health Magazine* and *Best Life Magazine*.

Chris is a Certified Strength and Conditioning Specialist and Certified Personal Trainer through the National Strength and Conditioning Association, and a Health Fitness Instructor and Advanced Personal Trainer through the American College of Sports Medicine. He also holds an Exercise and Pregnancy Instructor certification and is an American Red Cross Certified First Aid/CPR/AED Instructor. In addition, Chris is a full member of the NSCA, ACSM, British Association of Sport and Exercise Sciences, and the United Kingdom Strength and Conditioning Association.

Clinton Leo Greenstone, M.D.

Dr. Clinton Leo Greenstone received his medical degree from Yale University and his Internal Medicine training at the University of California San Francisco, where he also served as Chief Medical Resident. In 1990, his interest in education led him to join the faculty of the University of Chicago Pritzker School of Medicine. There Leo practiced and taught Internal Medicine, Medical Ethics and Evidence-Based Medicine and received numerous teaching awards for his efforts.

From 1994 to 2001, Leo practiced and taught Internal Medicine for the University of Michigan and its affiliate Oakwood Hospital, where he began incorporating lifestyle interventions and stress management techniques into his clinical and educational activities. As an advocate of humanistic medicine, he focused on the fact that health means a balanced life: body, mind and spirit.

The blending of conventional medical practices and unconventional lifestyle measures that help patients achieve optimal health has been coined "Integrative Medicine." Since 2001, Leo has been a leading teacher and practitioner in this new, exciting and important field. His strong conventional background in Internal Medicine, Clinical Medical Ethics, Evidence-Based Medicine combined with his humanistic patient-centered approaches make him a unique clinician educator. He truly is a physician for the future dedicated to bringing "health" and "care" back into the healthcare system.

From 2004 to 2006, Leo worked for Florida Hospital, a healthcare system dedicated to health and wellness. There he did Lifestyle Medicine research and directed the Rippe Health Assessment, an executive health assessment program. He continues to serve as a contributing editor of Dr. Rippe's *American Journal of Lifestyle Medicine*.

In 2006, Leo was appointed Assistant Clinical Professor of Medicine and Associate Chief of Staff for Ambulatory Care of the VA Ann Arbor Healthcare System, an affiliate institution of the University of Michigan. Since that time he has overseen the outpatient operations of the healthcare system, which includes community-based outpatient clinics in Jackson, Michigan, Flint, Michigan and Toledo, Ohio serving over 22,000 veterans. He also teaches clinical medicine to medical students and residents at the university.

Alan McMillan

In March 2001, Alan McMillan was elected as the President and CEO of the National Safety Council. Prior to becoming President, he had served for six years as the Executive Vice President and Chief Operating Officer at the Council. He has more than 40 years of government and private sector safety, health and environmental experience, including service with the U.S. Occupational Safety and Health Administration, and the Mine Safety and Health Administration.

Alan began his career in the Federal Government in 1966 at the Eglin Air Force Base in Fort Walton Beach, Florida. He joined the U.S. Department of Labor in 1970 as Regional Human Resources Director in Atlanta, Georgia. Alan later served as Chicago Regional Administrator of the Occupational Safety and Health Administration (OSHA) from 1981 to 1983 and was Administrator of OSHA's Atlanta region from 1983 to 1986. In 1987, he was named Acting Assistant Secretary of Labor for the U.S. Labor Department's Mine Safety and Health Administration and in 1988 became Deputy Assistant Secretary of Labor for Employment Standards.

From 1989 to 1992, Alan served as Deputy Assistant Secretary of Labor for the Occupational Safety and Health Administration where he was responsible for day-to-day OSHA operations including developing and implementing occupational safety and health standards, assisting workplaces through voluntary compliance programs and directing OSHA's nationwide enforcement responsibilities. In 1990, he received the Presidential Award for Distinguished Executive Service, the Federal government's highest award for senior executives.

In October 1992, Alan joined the Los Alamos National Laboratory in New Mexico where he led the organization's safety and health activities. He later assumed the position of Deputy Director of the Laboratory's Environmental, Safety, Health and Quality Programs.

Alan has served as a member of the Board of Directors for the Chicagoland Chamber of Commerce, the U.S./Mexico Chamber of Commerce, the Board of Directors of the Chicago Yacht Club, the Consumers Advisory Council of Underwriters Laboratory and the Board of Advisors to the Center for Business & Public Policy at Georgetown University in Washington, DC. He has also been a member of the Advisory Council to the Secretary of Energy for Environment, Safety and Health. He currently serves as an appointee of the Secretary of Labor as a member of the National Advisory Committee for Occupational Safety and Health (NACOSH).

Alan received his Bachelor of Science degree from the University of Florida in 1966 and his Master of Arts degree from the University of West Georgia in 1980. He also completed a Senior Executive Fellowship at Harvard University in 1980.

Fred Harburg

Fred Harburg is an Advisory Board member and keynote speaker for the Human Performance Institute. He is a respected consultant, writer and speaker in the disciplines of leadership, strategy and performance coaching.

Fred graduated from the U.S. Air Force Academy and served as an Air Force officer and pilot flying a variety of jet aircraft in both domestic and international missions, some of which were in direct support of the White House. He has a compelling personal history in highly demanding athletic, military and corporate settings. His wealth of successful experience enables him to credibly declare, "Organizations that intelligently equip their leaders to fully engage themselves and their people consistently outperform those that do not!"

Fred has held several significant international business leadership roles in the U.S. and abroad. He has been both an internal and external organizational architect for Fortune 100 companies including IBM, General Motors, Disney, AT&T and Fidelity Investments. He served as the Chief Learning Officer and President of Motorola University, which at its peak had over 1,000 faculty and staff members, and operated from more than 20 campuses around the world. His achievements at Motorola University were profiled in the November 2002 issue of *Chief Learning Officer Magazine*.

Fred's academic degrees include a Bachelor of Science from the U.S. Air Force Academy and a Master of Business Administration from the University of California, Los Angeles (UCLA). He served as a member of the Center for Effective Organizations Advisory Board at the Marshall School of Business, University of Southern California; is a member of the *Chief Learning Officer Magazine* Editorial Advisory Board, a publication for which he writes a bimonthly column on strategy; is an advisory board member for Tufts University Institute for Global Leadership; a Senior Fellow for The Trinity Forum; a guest lecturer at the MIT Sloan School of Management; and Director of PathNorth, a non-profit organization created for the purpose of encouraging principal business founders, owners and CEOs to broaden their definition of success. Fred has been interviewed by The Fox News Network on a range of issues dealing with effective leadership in challenging situations.

Jenny Evans

As a performance coach and keynote speaker for the Human Performance Institute, Jenny Evans trains hundreds of national and international corporate executives of Fortune 500 companies in energy management for increased productivity and performance. She specializes in both large and small group education and learning.

Jenny's professional experiences include being Founder and CEO of PowerHouse Wellness. As an international speaker, she promotes total employee health and well-being by educating executives on integrating body, mind and spirit. She has managed corporate wellness centers, produced an instructional yoga audio CD, taught various fitness classes and educated numerous employees on managing stress, nutrition and work-life balance. For the past 12 years, Jenny has also been involved in educating and training the public on overall wellness through frequent radio and television appearances. In addition, she is an aerial coach at Xelias Aerial Arts Studio.

Jenny holds a Bachelor of Science degree in Kinesiology with an emphasis in Psychology from the School of Kinesiology of the University of Minnesota. She is ACE certified as a personal trainer and group fitness instructor.

Jim Mellado

Jim Mellado is currently the President of the Willow Creek Association (WCA). He has been with the WCA for 16 years and has served as its President for the last 15 years. The WCA is celebrating its 16th anniversary and is now serving over 12,000 member churches from over 90 denominations around the world. Its mission is to envision, equip and encourage Christian leaders to build prevailing local churches. The vision is to see each church reaching its redemptive potential.

Jim is a 1991 graduate of the Harvard Business School. While a student at Harvard, he published a case study on the Willow Creek Community Church, which has become a part of the curriculum at the Harvard Business School, Stanford Business School, Northwestern's Kellogg School of Business and others.

In 1988, Jim competed in the Olympic Games in Seoul, South Korea and placed 26th of 42 athletes in the decathlon for the country of his birth, El Salvador. A year before that he competed in the Pan American Games and placed fourth in the decathlon competition.

Jim has a Mechanical Engineering undergraduate degree from Southern Methodist University in Dallas, Texas.

Rear Admiral Ray Smith, U.S. Navy (retired)

Widely regarded as one of the Navy's most inspirational leaders, Rear Admiral Ray Smith has spoken extensively on his leadership experiences to a wide range of audiences including corporate, political, military and civic leaders. A Navy SEAL for 31 years, he achieved extraordinary success through focused, participatory leadership. During his four-year tenure as Commander of the 2,300-men SEAL force, he raised personnel retention to a level three times the Navy average. As a Navy Captain, Ray led the Navy SEALs in Operation Desert Storm, conducting over 200 operations of strategic significance while incurring no casualties. Earlier in his career, he directed Navy SEAL training, generally considered to be the most challenging military training in the world.

Ray has been recognized in *Newsweek, Fortune, Reader's Digest*, and on the Discovery Channel, the History Channel and *CBS This Morning*. He published two highly successful Navy SEAL manuals, one on nutrition and one on fitness. He was awarded the California Distinguished Service Award while a member of the Governor's Council on Physical Fitness and Sports.

Ray was responsible for developing the Navy's first capability-based assessment process. He led 100 systems analysts in providing service-level recommendations directly to the Chief of Naval Operations. Incorporating computer modeling and risk assessment, he provided Navy leadership with US$36 billion in analysis-based savings over a six-year period.

Ray holds a Master of Science degree in Physical Oceanography from the U.S. Naval Postgraduate School in Monterey, California and a Bachelor of Science degree from the U.S. Naval Academy in Annapolis, Maryland. He successfully completed the 350-mile Beast of the East Adventure Race in 1998 and 1999, finishing with his three Navy SEAL teammates in 9th place out of 34 teams.

Will Marre

Will Marre is a Co-Founder and former President of the Covey Leadership Center. In his current role as CEO of ReaLeadership Alliance, he helps leaders identify, communicate and implement new socially-strategic models.

In 2004, Will founded The American Dream Project to help leaders of the future develop and find the ideas, tools and relationships they require to create the next chapter in American and world history. He recently received an Emmy Award® for writing the learning documentary *Reclaiming Your American Dream* that continues to air on public television stations around the country.

Will is a pioneer in socially-strategic enterprise. Working with New York Stock Exchange companies to combine charity and commerce, he co-founded the non-profit Seacology Foundation, the only conservation organization in the world expressly dedicated to saving the fragile environments and cultures of islanders, especially in the South Pacific. In a similar alliance, he co-founded Redline Revolution, an innovative non-profit educational organization aimed at reducing teenage deaths and accidents from car crashes.

Will is passionate about helping organizations to improve the quality of personal lives and accelerate economic and social improvement throughout the world. He is currently launching CitizenOne, an education campaign to teach social entrepreneurship to high school and college students worldwide.

About the
Human Performance Institute

The Human Performance Institute is the leader in energy management technology. Its technology of managing energy is measurement-based and is grounded in the sciences of performance psychology, exercise physiology and nutrition. The application of this technology has had a profound impact on performance and engagement in high-stress arenas, having successfully worked with a wide range of world-class performers from the worlds of business, sport, medicine, law enforcement, military Special Forces and FBI Hostage Rescue Teams. From its living laboratory of high stress, spanning more than 30 years, it has become clear that managing energy, not time, is the single most important factor in sustained high performance.

Headquartered in Orlando, Florida, the Human Performance Institute was co-founded by renowned performance psychologist Dr. Jim Loehr, author of 14 books including *The Power of Story* and co-author of the national bestseller *The Power of Full Engagement*, and Dr. Jack Groppel, internationally recognized authority on human performance, fitness and nutrition, and author of *The Corporate Athlete*.

HPI has developed the *Corporate Athlete Course* based on its multi-disciplinary energy management training system. Effectively managing energy requires training like an elite athlete—not an athlete in sport but a corporate athlete. Participants in the corporate athlete course actively train to increase their capacity at all levels—physically, emotionally, mentally and spiritually—to achieve sustained maximum performance in the face of unprecedented demands. Training solutions for both individuals and entire organizations include the corporate athlete course at HPI's headquarters in Orlando, Florida and at the United States Olympic Training Center in Colorado Springs, Colorado. Options also comprise on-site programs, train-the-trainer certification, client-led courses, keynote presentations by Jim Loehr, Jack Groppel and their team of highly credible performance coaches, as well as individual and organizational assessments and measurements. Corporate clients consist of an extensive array of Fortune 500 companies such as Procter & Gamble, GlaxoSmithKline, Dell, Allstate Insurance, PepsiCo, Citi, The Estée Lauder Companies and Nordstrom. Visit www.corporateathlete.com to learn more.